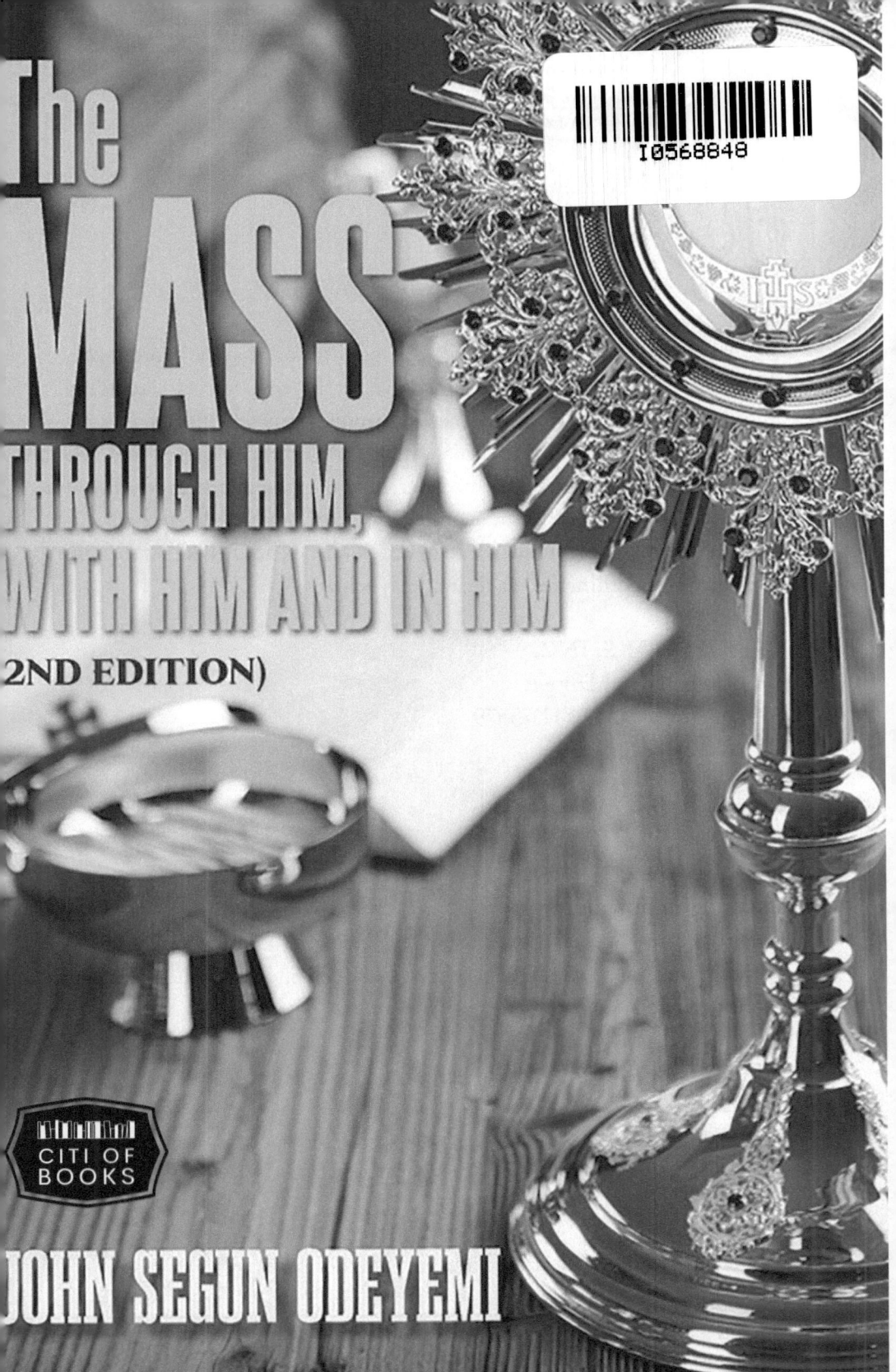

The
MASS
THROUGH HIM,
WITH HIM AND IN HIM
(2ND EDITION)

JOHN SEGUN ODEYEMI

CITIOFBOOKS, INC.
3736 Eubank NE Suite A1
Albuquerque, NM 87111-3579
www.citiofbooks.com

Hotline: 1 (877) 389-2759
Fax: 1 (505) 930-7244

Ordering Information:
Quantity sales. Special discounts are available on quantity purchases by corporations, associations, and others. For details, contact the publisher at the address above.

Printed in the United States of America.

ISBN-13:	Paperback	979-8-89391-445-0
	eBook	979-8-89391-446-7

Library of Congress Control Number: 2024923996

Dedication

This book is dedicated Ad Majoreim Dei Gloriam in Honor of
Most Rev. Dr. Ayo Maria Sunday Atoyebi OP
Emeritus Bishop of the Catholic Diocese of Ilorin, Nigeria.

Born: December 3, 1944

Final Religious Profession: December 8, 1974

Priestly Ordination: December 27, 1978

Episcopal Ordination: May 17, 1992

Episcopal Retirement: June 12, 2019

Table of Contents

Forward

We believe, as the Church teaches that at Mass Christ is made present under the sacramental species by transubstantiation, primarily and immediately as he is in himself. Thus, the Eucharist is the true Body and Blood of Jesus Christ, who is really and substantially present under the appearances of bread and wine, in order to offer himself in the sacrifice of the Mass and to be received as spiritual food in Holy Communion. The manner of his presence in the Eucharist is substantial, yet it is the whole Christ who is present. Furthermore, writing on the presence of Christ in the Eucharistic sacrifice, Charles Cardinal Journet, makes the case that it is the glorious Christ who is present at the Mass with his redemptive act. In his book *The Mass: The Presence of the Sacrifice of the Cross*, Journet writes, and it is worth quoting extensively:

> But if in heaven He continues to desire to save us, as He so desired once and for all by the very act of His Passion and His Death, it is in exactly this same way that He will be present to us at Mass. He will come in His glorious state; however, certainly not in order to touch us by His glory, but in order to "proclaim His death," to actualize according to our intention the unique act of redemption. He will come *with* His redemptive act. Between His glory and our sin, he will interpose His bloody Cross (p. 64).

From all this, a few things become clear: that the whole glorious Christ is present at Mass; that his redemptive act is made present to us once again – re-presented as it were at every Mass; and that we reap the benefits of his redemptive act of love.

Some further implications can be drawn from what is said here. In the first instance, it is true that the Mass cannot be celebrated as mere remembrance of an event that occurred over two thousand years ago. In other words, that the Mass is not just a symbol of the redemptive act of Christ; rather, that each time we celebrate the sacrifice of the Mass, we are placed in that very redemptive act, where the saving love of Jesus Christ which was made manifest on the Cross of Calvary is lavished upon us. In this regard, the sacrifice on

Calvary and the sacrifice of the Mass are not two different sacrifices, but the one sacrifice of Christ Jesus. On the cross of Calvary, the sacrifice was bloody, but at Mass, the same sacrifice is offered in an unbloody manner. Moreover, the Last Supper was not another sacrifice than that of the Cross; it was the very same sacrifice of the Cross, already begun at that hour and made present, as it would need to be henceforth, under the appearances of bread and wine. It is the same Christ who was offered at the Last Supper, on the Cross, and who is offered at Mass. At the Last Supper, he was offered to be immolated; on the Cross, he was offered in immolation; and at Mass, he is offered as immolated.

If this then is the nature of the Mass, any attempt to reflect on it, to understand it, and to consequently help us relish its rich meaning for our lives in order to reap the benefits of the redemptive act of Christ, can never be superfluous. For this reason, the effort of the author of this book is worthwhile. His desire to reflect on the mystery of God's love for us in the Mass has motivated him to work on this project. I do, however, see another profound motivation for this work. The author indicated that the book is written to coincide and to honor Most Rev. Ayo-Maria Atoyebi, OP., Bishop Emeritus of the Catholic Diocese of Ilorin. This gesture brings out the beautiful correlation between the Priesthood and the Eucharist. The Eucharist is "the source and summit of the Christian life" (*Lumen Gentium*, 11). "The other sacraments, and indeed all ecclesiastical ministries and works of the apostolate, are bound up with the Eucharist and are oriented toward it. For in the blessed Eucharist is contained the whole spiritual good of the Church, namely Christ himself, our Pasch" (*Presbyterorum ordinis*, 5). Therefore, because the Priesthood and the Eucharist are ordered one to another, to present a book the Mass in honor of a bishop on the 40th anniversary of his priestly ordination is not a mere coincidence. The book itself highlights the correlation between the Priesthood and the Mass.

The book makes a significant reference to the fact that the Mass makes present the redemptive act of Christ by looking at the Jewish roots of the Last Supper. The *Catechism of the Catholic Church* teaches, "By celebrating the Last Supper with his apostles in the course of the Passover meal, Jesus gave the Jewish Passover its definitive meaning. Jesus' passing over to his father by his death and Resurrection, the new Passover, is anticipated in the Supper and celebrated in the Eucharist, which fulfills the Jewish Passover and anticipates the final Passover of the Church in the glory of the kingdom" (*CCC* 1340). Thus, the Eucharist (Mass) is the memorial of Christ's Passover, the making present and the sacramental offering of his unique sacrifice, in the liturgy of the Church, which is his Body. It is, indeed, a sacrifice because it re-presents (makes present) the sacrifice of the Cross, because it is its memorial and because it applies its fruit. The attempt of the author to reflect on every part of the Mass in this book will help the reader to appreciate the beauty of the Mass as making present the redemptive act of Christ's love. It will also serve as a useful guide for celebrating and actively participating in the sacrifice of the Holy Mass.

Very Rev. Fr. Francis 'Kunle Adedara, STL, Ph.D
Dean of Studies
Seminary of Ss. Peter and Paul,
Ibadan, Nigeria

ACKNOWLEDGEMENT

I am grateful to God for the inspiration to undertake this work and most of all, for the courage and strength to see it through despite a grueling work schedule and other deadlines. Deep in my heart, I know this effort will bless one person somewhere in the world and bring them closer to the Lord Jesus present in the Eucharist. This work started out as a parish catechesis in the weekly parish bulletin. I had worked on a four part one paragraph a week with my pastoral collaborators at St. Bartholomew Parish, Penn Hills; Melissa Busbey(RIP) and Bess Biamonte. I am grateful for the many ways in which these women supported my ministry while I was at St. Barth's.

I am indebted to my brother priests, Very Rev. Frs. Lou Vallone, and Carmen D'Amico, both of whom have been a guiding light for me in the diocese of Pittsburgh. I owe a huge debt of gratitude to Very Rev. Fr. Francis Kunle Adedara, Ph.D, who read my manuscript, provided very helpful editorial suggestions, granted the much-needed nihil Obstat, and graciously provided a forward for this book. Same sentiment is extended to Very Rev. Fr. Anselm K. Jimoh, Ph.D, who single handedly supervised the publication of the first edition of this text. I appreciate the kindness of Very Rev. Fr. James B. Owolagba, JCD, judicial vicar of the Archdiocese of Regina, Canada, for his editorial advice and for providing a book back blurb comment. Thanks to Very Rev. Fr. Ezekiel ade Owoeye, (RIP) parish priest of Our Lady Seat of Wisdom, University of Ibadan, Nigeria for all his encouragement and support. My appreciation goes to Very Rev. Fr. Anthony Taiye Fadairo, parish priest of St. Agnes Church, Maryland, Lagos, for his willingness always to step up to the plate when no one else will. I thank Irene Lahr, MA, for offering thorough editorial advice. For this second edition, I thank Mr. Tom Sobotie who did a total review of the entire manuscript for this second edition.

I thank all my friends who accept me unconditionally and support me to strive always to always be a better version of myself. I thank all those who remember me in their prayers and entrust themselves to mine. One of the saddest things I experience as a Catholic Christian and priest is when former Catholics fall away from the sacraments. I ask that in your prayers, as you read this book;

kindly pray for all lapsed Catholics and the possibility of Eucharistic unity of Christians. The Eucharist is the greatest gift of all; let us approach this great gift with all gratitude and thankfulness.

Oh Sacrament most Holy, Oh Sacrament Divine; All praise and all Thanksgiving be every moment thine!

JSO

For I received from the Lord what I also passed on to you: The Lord Jesus, on the night he was betrayed, took bread, and when he had given thanks, he broke it and said, "This is my body, which is for you; do this in remembrance of me." In the same way, after supper he took the cup, saying, "This cup is the new covenant in my blood; do this, whenever you drink it, in remembrance of me." For whenever you eat this bread and drink this cup, you proclaim the Lord's death until he comes.

(1Cor. 11:23-32)

Introduction: What is mass?

Over the years, I have had various opportunities across a vast range of persons and cultures and across many international boundaries to engage in the conversations of what religion means, or what does the Catholic priesthood mean, what is confession!? My favorite of all times is whenever the conversation shifts to the meaning of the Catholic Mass. It is interesting to note that even self-avowed atheists and agnostics are at least vaguely aware of the fact that the Catholic Mass carries some significance, which is subjectable to debate and analysis. On a more contemporary level, I have devoted some time attempting to explain in the simplest ways possible, the hidden meanings behind the structure of the liturgy of the celebration of Holy Mass. A theological explanation, often times, does not go well. In the light of our present and somewhat rude awakening, declining numbers in Church attendance in the west and with the proliferation of Churches due to the impact of Pentecostalism, finding new methods and hermeneutical means of bringing the riches of the Eucharist to all is of great importance. No one needs a crystal ball or need to become a rocket scientist to agree that all over the world, the Catholic Church is impacted in different ways with waves and waves of secularism, ultra-modernism and anti-clericalism (which to some extent is self-inflicted).

In Europe and America, the numbers keep dropping dramatically forcing many dioceses to close down and sell Church buildings. The decrease in the number of men and women religious in these regions also is not helping. In the global South, while the number of Christians is on an upward surge, there is a problem of proliferation and mushrooming of new Christian Evangelical/Charismatic/Pentecostal groups. It will also seem that these various new impulses are not overly concerned with evangelizing un-evangelized persons but making proselytization part of their mission. I was in shock some time ago when I was home in Nigeria on vacation and a brother priest had mentioned a new phenomenon; they had Catholics who came to Mass and right from Mass go straight to a Pentecostal Church. Upon further investigation, the priest gathered that most people come to the Catholic Church for the Eucharist and go to the Pentecostal Church to "be fed" with the word!

As I continue to reflect on Catholicism and its natural encounter with modernity that proclaims science as God, or the global south where there is babbling of religiosity marked with corruption in high places, ignorance and poverty, I am forced to ask repeatedly; how is the Catholic Church failing to reach the core of modern-day men and women? The Catholic Church holds a tradition that goes in an unbroken line back to the apostolic Church. The Catholic Church singly has shown through time and the struggle against schisms, heresies, and modernity, to remain true to apostolic traditions, the early Church found in the book of the Acts of the Apostles and to Patristic traditions and the living magisterium.[1] For this, the Church has been ridiculed and castigated as being ancient and out of touch with modern realities. In my reflections, I have concluded that one of the ways to encounter people in a much-needed re-evangelization of peoples, there is a need to make the sacraments appealing to everyday persons. Scholastic theology is foundational to understanding the sacraments; however, to convince anyone in our time, a simplified explanation of the little things helps to make better meaning of what people really celebrate in faith. Baptism is the foundation of all the sacraments, and rightly so. The Eucharist remains at the center and holds the other sacraments together. It contains in itself the entire economy of the history of human salvation in and through Jesus Christ; the mother sacrament to which all other sacraments are directed and receive life from.

In this simple book, I consciously chose a methodology of approaching the greatest mystery of all couched in mundane and simple language. While trying to espouse how best to make full use of some of the inherent traditions behind what happens as we prepare for Holy Mass, during mass and after Mass, without becoming too pedantic. Before you get into exploring the beauty and riches of the Mass in this book, I would like to clarify the very nature of what the Catholic liturgy of the Mass is, different from what many may assume it is.

---

[1] The four characteristics of the Catholic faith is contained in the creed; the Church is one, holy, catholic and apostolic. Christ bestowed these gifts upon His Church through the Holy Spirit. These marks make the Church what it is and not depending upon either on the institution or its hierarchy and people.

The celebration of Mass is at the heart of our worship as an ecclesial community. Jesus instituted the Eucharistic sacrifice, the banquet of divine love, at the Last Supper. We need to remember that the Eucharist is the summit and source of our Christian life. Why? Because in the Eucharist is found the entire treasure of the Church—Jesus Christ truly present in His body, soul and divinity under the appearance of bread and wine. The Eucharist is the memorial of Christ's life, saving death, and Resurrection made present for our salvation in the liturgy. Christ, acting through the ministry of his priests, is both the priest offering the sacrifice and the victim being offered in sacrifice. As sacrifice, the Eucharist is also offered in reparation for the sins of the living and the dead; to obtain spiritual and temporal benefits from God. To receive communion, one should be in a state of grace. A person conscious of mortal sin may not receive Communion until absolved from their sins by a priest who has the Church's mandate and authority to confer absolution in the Sacrament of Penance. The fruits of Holy Communion include a deeper union with Christ, a closer identity with all the faithful, a commitment to the poor, and a pledge of future glory. The faithful are urged to receive Communion at every Mass they attend and participate fully. This includes the opportunity to receive Christ in the Eucharist more than once on the same day. The Eucharist is a communion with Christ, with our brothers and sisters and the entire universal Church. It is also a communion with the Church of the saints, triumphant in heaven. Let us always prayerfully prepare for Mass, celebrate by participating fully at Mass, and take the fruits of the Mass with us as we go. Every time we gather for Mass, we obey the Lord's instruction; **"Do this in memory of me"**. (Mt. 26:26-28, Mk. 14:12-25, Lk. 22:7-22)

The Mass, wherever it is celebrated is a universal action of the Church in which earth calls on heaven and heaven lifts up earth. At Mass, the divine infuses grace and presence into humanity. The Church militant, the Church suffering and the Church triumphant are all linked in this one sacred act of worship where glory is given to God and graces are poured upon humanity. The Mass is fully alive when people gather and the Church prays using the word, breaking bread and sharing in the one cup of the blood of Jesus. The 'Eucharist'-the sacrifice of Holy Mass is a living sacrifice of Christ on the cross now rendered in an unbloody manner on the altar. The sacrifice of Mass is not merely symbolic of Christ' suffering and death on the cross, rather, the Mass makes Christ present sacramentally within His redeeming work on the cross to everyone who participates in this celebration The Eucharist is the real presence of Jesus among His own people under the appearance of bread and wine. In addition, in the Eucharist, we enter in communion with the Lord and with all those who profess His name and are conjoined all around the altars of the world. As we shall reflect on later, it is essential to delineate the foundational aspect of sacrifice from two perspectives: the Passover meal of Judaic origins and the words of Jesus at the institution of the Eucharist. The notion of a 'body offered up and blood poured out' recalls aspects of Jewish sacrificial rites in which the body of an animal is offered up and its blood poured forth. We see this laid out at the Passover in Egypt and at Mount Sinai. Christ becomes the new lamb of sacrifice who gives completely the gift of himself, in body, soul and divinity. The term 'Lamb of God' will also be examined so that the sacrifice of the new covenant shows that the Messiah has come and remains with us. The Mass is the new covenant sealed in the blood of the Lamb, poured out for many for the forgiveness of sins, to be celebrated in perpetuity and in memory of the Lord.

According to Edward Sri,

> ...the Jewish notion of memorial... does not merely recall a past event. It makes that event present. Therefore, when Jesus said, 'Do this in memory of me,' he was commanding the apostles to make present as a biblical memorial the sacrifice of his body and blood at the last supper. Indeed, the body and blood Jesus spoke of at the last supper is his body and blood that was sacrificed on Calvary, and this is what is made present to us at mass.[2]

The late eminent American Catholic Theologian, Avery Cardinal Dulles, buttresses this point further as he clarified, "...the biblical notion of *anamnesis* (Hebrew *zikkaron*) supports the teaching of the council of Trent that the Eucharist is not a mere recalling (*nuda*

---

[2] Edward Sri. *A Biblical Walk Through the Mass: Understanding what we say and do in the liturgy.* (Westchester, Pennsylvania: Ascension Press, 2011), Pp. 5-6

commemoration, DS 1753) of what Christ did in the past. Memorial in the rich biblical sense meant a liturgical feast commemorating some foundational event in such a way that the people participate by faith in its saving effects."[3]

Dulles sums up this teaching in very clear terms, and I will adopt this approach as I attempt to lead the reader through the meaning and mystery of the Holy Mass.

> The Catholic position on the Eucharist as sacrifice... combines strong biblical realism with ecclesial personalism. It insists on the intrinsic connection among the sacrifice of Christ on the cross, the sacrificial meal of the Last Supper, the liturgical sacrifice of the Church, and the personal sacrifice of those who participate. The Church and its members are privileged not only to receive the fruits of Christ's redemptive sacrifice but also to take part, according to their respective offices and vocations, in the supreme act of Christ's own priestly ministry... As a manifestation of what the Church is called to be, it builds up the Church here on earth as a sign of the living Christ. As a prelude to the heavenly liturgy, it quickens the Church's hope for the age to come. The sacrifice, therefore, is as a memorial of the passion, an offering of the church today, and a foretaste of the New Jerusalem.[4]

The Eucharist is the *real presence* of Jesus among His people; in His words (scripture), in the assembly of those gathered (the Church), in the poor, but more so in the Eucharist where Jesus makes himself truly and wholly present. He is the same Emmanuel – God who is with us, present to us and always for us. One of the miracles of the Eucharist is that at the reception of Holy Communion, Jesus enters, unworthy as we may be, into the recipient and becomes intimately part of the person. This is the reason why one of the ancient prayers of the saints at communion is that "we may become

[3] Avery Dulles. "The Eucharist as sacrifice." In Roch A. Kereszty (ed.) *Rediscovering the Eucharist: Ecumenical Conversations.* (NY/Mahwah, NJ: Paulist Press,3003), P. 178

[4] Ibid. P.185

what we have received." Perhaps many do not fully grasp that at the celebration of all Masses, according to Saint John Paul II, it is a mysterious participation in a heavenly liturgy!

Though most of us in the western and southern hemisphere are familiar with the Roman rite Mass, within the Catholic Church there are various other rites of celebrating the Mass; like the Ambrosian and Mozarabic rites found mostly in Milan, Italy. There is the Byzantine rite celebrated by Orthodox Catholics in the East, the Coptic rite in North Africa, the Syro Malabar in some parts of India. We have the Maronite rite from Lebanon and the Zairean rite from East Africa. Whatever rite is celebrated, the underlying theology is the same; Jesus is truly present in the bread and wine that are consecrated and in the reception of Holy Communion, we truly receive the body and blood of Christ.

In the Church, we generally speak of the Mass when it is referred to as the Eucharist, which means thanksgiving. In the early Church, it was popularly referred to as the 'breaking of bread' and 'the Lord's Supper.' In contemporary times, we speak often of the Holy Mass. The sacrifice of Holy Mass is to be celebrated in perpetuity as a reenactment of the institution of the Eucharist, the new and eternal covenant, sealed by the blood of Christ on the cross. With this gift of Himself, on Holy Thursday night, the Lord reimagined for us the gift of the sacred priesthood, which is to serve the Eucharist and other sacraments of the Church. The Lord Jesus also established the role of service both for priests and for the Christian people by showing us the example of washing each other's feet. The Eucharist as the sacrifice of Christ is intrinsically bound to the priesthood, and the rule of love and service. As a post-ressurectional act of worship, Jesus commanded his disciples "Do this in memory of me." (cf. Lk. 22:19) Dulles states,

> The mass, as an 'unbloody' sacrifice, is not a repetition of what Christ did once and for all on Calvary, but a ritual reactualization that once for all act, no less than the anticipation of that act at the last supper. The sacramental sacrifice, unlike the sacrifice of the cross, is repeatable. It is not a mere imitation of the archetypal sacrifice of Jesus but that same sacrifice

mysteriously renewed after the event... The mass is a work of divine power that surpasses anything in the natural order. In a manner that defies human comprehension, the Holy Spirit makes it possible for Christ's redemptive act, without loss of its historical uniqueness, to be available to all ages.[5]

The Mass is certainly not a place to be entertained. One of the regular complaints I hear especially in Europe, America, and from many ex-Catholics of African descent is that the Mass is boring. I put this down to the fact that we now live in a world suffused and inundated by celluloid and audio entertainment. Most people are "plugged-in" to some kind of device or the other from morning until night. Contemporary times continue to evolve away from meditation, contemplation, and times of introspection. The constancy with which our eardrums and brains are bombarded with information makes any significant period of silence uncomfortable – or boring. Unwittingly but unfortunately, the newer Christian religious movements glory in the music, performances, glitterati, and "feel-good" acts of worship. It has become commonplace to find in these new Christian movements comedians and performers invited to make appearances during Sunday worship. What they claim is their sanctuary, or altar (without sacrifice) thus becomes a stage for a show, simply to fulfil the entertainment value for which many crave. I personally argue that without good music, without an excellent homilist, yet, with the proper disposition and self-discipline to listening to the words at the readings of sacred scripture at Mass and the words of consecration, an active and spiritually fulfilling Mass can be experienced. This is not to say good liturgical music and an excellent homily are not needed, I insist that without both, we should still encounter the divine and the sublime at Mass. Sometimes, it is not simply a question of what you get out of mass; but also what did you put into it, in terms of your attention, and full participation?

When the sacred liturgy of the Mass is properly celebrated with its required solemnity and dignity, the attendees at Mass experience the sacredness of the moment. Solemnity and dignity must always be accorded to the celebration of the Eucharist. There are various moments and movements at mass that allow us to experience

---

[5] Avery Dulles."The Eucharist as Sacrifice." Op.Cit. Pp.199-80

joy, contrition, praise, worship, reception and blessings all within this one moment. We can celebrate the Mass joyfully and make it uplifting with guitars and drums, but with great care that it does not degenerate into entertainment or mere 'feel-good' and crowd pleaser gathering. It is the duty of the presiding priest or chief celebrant to prepare for the liturgy, and then help the people to enter into the sacred moment of the liturgy. He is to lead them prayerfully through the celebration, and then send them forth to live the life of grace they have received through word and sacrament.

The Eucharist is the center and summit of the Catholic prayer life. It is the gift that is both food for our lives' journey and a pledge for everlasting life. There are two things that saddens me the most in the Catholic Church; to find a priest who does not celebrate this great mystery as solemnly as possible, and when I find Catholics who fall away from the Church and sacraments – especially the Holy Eucharist. The words of Jesus in the scriptures cannot be explained away by any exegesis. They are what Jesus says they are,

> I am the bread of life. Your fathers ate manna in the desert, and they are dead; but this is the bread, which comes down from heaven, so that a person may eat it and not die. I am the living bread, which comes down from heaven. Anyone who eats this bread will live forever; and the bread that I shall give is my flesh, for the life of the world... In truth, I tell you, if you do not eat the flesh of the son of man and drink his blood, you have no life in you. Anyone who does eat my flesh and drink my blood has eternal life, and I shall raise that person up on the last day. For my flesh is real food and my blood is real drink. Whoever eats my flesh and drinks my blood lives in me and I in that person. As the Father sent me, and I draw life from the Father, so whoever eats me will also draw life from me. This is the bread, which has come down from heaven; it is not like the bread our ancestors ate: they are dead, but anyone who eats this bread will live forever. (Jn. 6:47-51, 53-58)

I have desired for a long time to write a biblical and theological investigation of what the Mass means, especially with its antecedent connections with our "older brother" in the faith; Judaism. No true Christian/Catholic can ignore the connections we have to Judaism. As long as we claim Abraham as our father in faith, we hold as sacred the Ten Commandments. We are bound also into the covenantal people of God, sons and daughters of a promise; from the Abrahamic covenant in Genesis 12:1-3, the Mosaic in Exodus 19:5-6, the Davidic covenant in 2 Samuel 7. We then encounter the covenants with the prophets; Jeremiah, Isaiah, and Ezekiel in which the established nation of Israel is promised a Messiah through whom all the nations of the earth will know the true God. Jesus is the fulfillment of all the covenants God made with Israel. In the celebration of the Eucharist, our faith is bound to the Judaic traditions through the covenants concluded in Christ- the bread of life. The words of Jesus explain our connection when he said, "I have not come to abolish the law and the prophets, but to bring them to fulfilment." (Mt. 5:17)

The Mass and the Book of Revelation

Dr. Scott Hahn, Catholic convert, theologian and Catholic apologist in his highly successful book, *The Lamb's Supper: The Mass as Heaven on Earth* gives very useful insights into the connections between various allegories employed in the writings of John in the book of Revelation. This work considers some of the insights in the work of Scott Hahn to shed light on these historical and foundational backgrounds to the Mass. In his first encounter with the Catholic Mass, a protestant pastor, curious young academic, Hahn writes that the first thing that struck him at his 'first mass' was the use of titles for Christ but more specifically, the reference to Christ as *The Lamb of God*. Recognizing the various titles of Christ, Lord, God, Savior, Messiah, King, Priest, Prophet – all refer to the God-man, titles of dignity, wisdom, power and status – but The Lamb of God? Lambs do not represent the most powerful or admired of animals. Perhaps this is why one can feel a sense of immense power when Jesus is referred to in Revelation 5:5 as *The Lion of Judah*. According to Hahn, "… the Lion of Judah makes only a cameo appearance in the book of Revelation. Meanwhile, the Lamb dominates, appearing no less than twenty-eight times. The Lamb rules, occupying heaven's throne (Rev. 22:3). It is the Lamb who leads an army of hundreds of thousands of men and angels, striking fear in the hearts of the wicked (Rev. 6:15-16)."[6]

At the beginning of the book of Revelation, in John's vision, and based on the invitation of an elder, no one can open the seal. The elder then encourages John, "Weep not; lo, the Lion of the tribe of Judah, the root of David, has conquered, so that He can open the scroll and its seven seals." (Rev.5:5) John then looks for a lion but instead he sees a Lamb – as though slain! The elders (*presbyteroi*-priests) then sing, "Worthy are You to take the scroll and to open its seals, for you were slain, and by your blood You ransomed men for God." (Rev. 5:9) At which heaven and earth responds, "To Him who sits upon the throne and to the Lamb be blessing and honor and glory and might for ever and ever! ... and the elders fell down and worshipped." (Rev. 5:13-14) The Catholic Church teaches in words and symbols that Jesus the Christ is the Lamb of God, crucified, risen, the high priest of the one true sanctuary, He who offers Himself and is offered, Who gives and is given. In many works of art, from stained glass windows to altar clothes, hymn books, etc., we often see a lamb carrying a flag of victory yet pierced and still bleeding. The Catholic Church recognizes Jesus along with John the Baptist and precursor of the Lord when he cried out, "Behold, the Lamb of God!" (cf. Jn. 1:36)

Hahn, following the traditions of the Old Testament links the Lamb to sacrifice, one of the primal forms of worship.[7] Out of all these sacrifices, Hahn points at two that deserve careful attention; the sacrifice of Melchizedek (Gen. 14:18-20), and the sacrifice of Abraham and Isaac. (Gen. 22) Melchizedek is a figure with no antecedents; a priest and king who foreshadows Christ. As King of 'Salem', later to be known as Jerusalem meaning the city of peace. Jesus will one day become the King of the new Jerusalem as the 'Prince of Peace.' Of particular importance is to note that in Melchizedek's sacrifice, it involved no animal. The Priest-King of

---

[6] Scott Hahn. *The Lamb's Supper: The Mass as Heaven on Earth.* (New York: Doubleday Publishing, 1999), Pp. 14-15

[7] From the earliest account of scripture, sacrifice dominates the landscape; Cain and Abel (Gen. $:3-4), the burnt offering of Noah (Gen. 8:20-21), the sacrifice of Abraham (Gen15:8-10; 22:13) and the sacrifice of Jacob (Gen. 46:1) The Genesis account is full of altars, sacrifices and wine libations.

Salem offered bread and wine and ended with a blessing on Abraham. It was at this same site at Salem that Abraham would respond to the directives of God for him to sacrifice Isaac, his only son. Abraham stands resolute and is going to do the will of God but God stays his hands and provides in place of Isaac, a lamb for the sacrifice. Here, God makes a covenant with Abraham and his descendants. Later on in Christian history, biblical scholars will reread all of these events and find corollaries,

- The story of Abraham and Isaac is allegorical to that of Jesus; while God spares Isaac – an only child, God does not spare His own only son but offers Him for the salvation of the world.

- Just like Isaac, Jesus will have to carry the wood for the sacrifice up a hill, the site for both events associated with Jerusalem.

- In the genealogy found in Mt. 1:1, Jesus is identified, like Isaac, to be a 'son of Abraham.'

- Abraham is understood to have prophesied about the Messiah when he responded to his son Isaac who had asked where the lamb was to be sacrificed, "God will provide Himself, the Lamb, for a burnt offering." (Gen.22:8) This Lamb is Jesus.

As the history of Israel's covenantal relationship continued down through the ages, Israel as a nation makes another sacrifice, which will lead to a new covenant: the Passover. In this act of deliverance from slavery in Egypt, the Israelites sacrificed a pure Lamb, which redeemed every first born of the house of the Jews on whose doorpost the blood of the Lamb was smeared. In this redemptive action, God consecrated Israel as a 'kingdom of priests, a holy nation... a nation God called His own firstborn son.' (Ex. 19:6, 4:22) After the liberation from Egypt, God commanded that the Passover be celebrated annually for all times as a remembrance *(Anamnesis)* of God's salvation to His people. Israel's sacrifices will be placed within the context of the Temple built around 960 BC. Hahn avers, "The Jerusalem Temple brought together all the strains that had gone before. Built on the site where Melchizedek had offered bread and wine, and where Abraham had offered his son, and where God had sworn His oath to save all nations, the temple served as the enduring place of offerings, principal of which was identical with that most ancient sacrifice of Abel: the lamb."[8] Jesus celebrated the sacrificed lamb at the Passover as part of His cultural and religious practices. It was not optional, since through the covenant Israel made with God, to remain a faithful Jew was to participate in this rite and explain it to one's children and they in turn to their own children.

Jesus will transpose the meaning of the Passover into the Eucharist and the evangelists and Epistle writers all will apply allegories to support this notion. For instance, in the gospel of John, he notes that Jesus was brought bound before Pilate at the sixth hour. (cf. Jn. 19:14) John was thinking of the same sixth hour when the priests were beginning to slaughter the Passover lamb. John makes explicit reference to the fact that the bones of Jesus were not broken after his death on the cross. It is a direct reference to Ex. 12:46, which states that the Lamb for the Passover must not have any broken bones. John finds another parallel by taking note that Jesus was given vinegar on hyssop to drink on the cross. It was the hyssop branch required for the sprinkling of the sacrificed lamb to mark the doorposts of the Jews at the first Passover. John also referenced the garment of Jesus sewn from top to bottom using the same word that referred to the vestment of the high priest. In addition, perhaps to some extent, the curtain in the temple covering the Holy of Holies, which was torn from top to bottom at the hour Jesus expired on the cross. (cf. Mt. 27:51) Some exegetes also see symbolically that the curtain is torn to reveal the Holy of Holies to all and no longer just the high priests. The same event concluded Levitical priesthood as it was known; it ushered in the priesthood of Jesus who is the priest per excellence.

Referencing Paul's first letter to the Corinthians, Hahn shows that the mass is the new Passover, "Christ, our paschal lamb, has been sacrificed. Let us therefore celebrate the festival… with unleavened bread of sincerity and truth." (cf. 1Cor. 5:7-8, 10:15-21, 11:23-32) Hahn places emphasis on this evolution,

---

[8] Scott Hahn. *The Lamb's Supper*… Op.Cit. Pp. 21-2

It is not enough that Christ bled and died for our sake. Now we have our part to play. As with the old Covenant, so with the new. If you want to mark your covenant with God, to seal your covenant with God, to renew your covenant with God, *you must eat the Lamb*... It begins to sound familiar. 'Unless you eat the flesh of the Son of man and drink His blood, you have no life in you. (Jn. 6:54) ... Man's primal need to worship God has always expressed itself in sacrifice: worship that is simultaneously an act of praise, atonement, self-giving, covenant, and thanksgiving (in Greek, *Eucharistia*)... Our supreme act of worship is a supreme act of sacrifice: the Lamb's Supper, the Mass.[9]

The liturgy of the Mass is experienced all through the senses; smell, touch, taste, sight, and hearing. The liturgy is practical, physical, psychological, and spiritual. It is impossible to encounter the riches of the sacrament of the Lamb of God without making an effort to learn, pray, and meditate on the sacred celebration. The Mass is pure joy when the priest greets his people; *'The Lord be with you,'* when he invites them, *'Lift up your heart.'* Our hearts leap in our chests when he presents the gospel to us, when we pray the creed, when he receives our gifts at the offertory to be brought up with the bread and wine. We are joined with elders/presbyteroi in the courts of heaven when we proclaim, *'The Lamb of God who takes away the sins of the world, have mercy on us.'* Then the bridegroom comes, lifted up, the priest invites us, *'Behold the Lamb of God, who takes away the sins of the world...'* At that moment, like Thomas, in our hearts, we whisper, humbly and on our knees, the words of Thomas; *'My Lord and my God.'* According to Hahn, "Though the actions are many, the mass is *one offering,* and that is the sacrifice of Jesus Christ, which renews our covenant with God the Father."[10]

I have come across various books written on different aspects of the Mass that for a while, I put the idea to rest asking what new perspective can I add? Until when the auspicious occasion for the celebration of the 40th anniversary of the priestly ordination and the

---

[9] Scott Hahn. *The Lamb's Supper*... Op.Cit. P.28
[10] Ibid. P.43

26th anniversary of the episcopal ordination of Most Rev. Dr. Ayo Maria Atoyebi, OP, Catholic Bishop of Ilorin was muted and marked for celebration. (He is now Bishop Emeritus.) I felt it befitting to publish this book in his honor. His dedication to the Eucharist and love for the Blessed Mother is well known. In his ministry as Bishop of Ilorin, and over the years, I have heard him encourage our people to be devoted to our Lord in the Eucharist, and to regularly pay visits to our Lord in the Blessed Sacrament. To attend Benediction and always pray the rosary. He does not only talk the talk, he shows all by the example of his own life, this commitment. By his efforts, cajoling and encouragement, I doubt if there is a single Church in the various parishes of our diocese without daily adoration and Benediction before morning Mass. And in many of our parishes where the facilities are available, the opportunity exists for all day exposition and adoration. It is, therefore, only befitting that this work is dedicated to him and with the greater hope that it does enlighten Catholics and Christians who seek to understand the Eucharist which we will continue to celebrate until the Lord returns; **Through Him, with him and in Him.**

Fr. John Segun Odeyemi
November 1, 2024
Feast of All Saints

Chapter One: Preparing for Mass

"I was glad when they said to me let us go up with joy, to the house of the Lord." (Ps. 122:1)

As Catholics, we believe our Churches are sacred spaces; God's own house, to which He invites all His people, where they may go to give thanks, offer their prayers and worship to their God and Creator. Like any house to which one is invited, there is always some sort of basic etiquette or rules, and God's house is no different. I will offer below some basic rules to help you feel at home in the Church, which preserves the solemnity of a sacred place and allows others to pray and worship in the right atmosphere. As simple and as obvious as some of these remarks may seem to some, it is true that people seem to forget the most obvious. I have also encountered many well-intentioned people, priests and consecrated/ religious included, who 'adjust' or consider some of the following unnecessary. However, note that these rules are formulated in line with what the Church has always taught considering the Church as a holy place of worship and the expected demeanor at the celebration of the Church's liturgies.

Preparation for Mass in a real devotional sense should start during the week. One of the best ways to be prepared for going to Mass, either daily or Sunday Masses, is to have encountered the readings ahead of time. In some parishes, bible study during the week focuses on reading the scriptural texts for the following Sunday with members sharing their personal reflections and always under the guidance of a capable leader or the priest himself. The Catholic Church encourages the daily reading of scriptures as part of personal, family prayers and devotions. In the case of single people or people who live alone, the practice of *lectio divina* - praying with the scriptures are encouraged. This aspect of preparing to enter the sacred liturgy must not be allowed to die; it is a tradition that builds our encounter with Jesus in His words and our encounter with him at Mass. Remember, St. Jerome says, "Ignorance of scripture is ignorance of Christ."

Another level of preparation, which is absolutely necessary, is the examen. An examination of conscience; to sincerely see if one needs to go to confession due to mortal sin. In the case of venial sins, we could make a sincere heart of contrition with a firm commitment to going to confession as soon as it is possible. One must also remember that doing penance as prescribed by the priest is necessary for completing a good celebration of the sacrament of reconciliation. However, in some cases, going to reconciliation at penance may also require us to seek reconciliation with anyone with whom we may have had a falling out. Jesus makes it clear in the scriptures "if you bring your gift to the altar of God and you realize in your heart that a brother has something against you, leave your gift and first go and be reconciled to your brother before offering your gift to God." (Mt. 5:24) The ideal of forgiveness, mercy and reconciliation is a prerequisite for a meaningful and fruitful celebration of the Holy Mass.

Fast before Mass. It is Church law that one fast for at least 1 hour before receiving Holy Communion. Water and medicine may be consumed, of course. The purpose is to help us prepare to receive Jesus in the Eucharist. As much as it possible, we should avoid bringing food and drink into Church. Sometimes, people who are ill or on particular kind of medication may need rehydration, this is permissible. The exceptions would be a drink for little children, water for the priest or choir (if discreet) and water for those who are ill. Bringing a snack into church is not appropriate, because we want to set the church apart as a place of prayer and reflection.

Show up at least a few minutes early. Getting to Mass early allows you to pray and prepare yourself better for Mass. It is always helpful to have a few minutes of quiet time to compose oneself mentally and be spiritually ready to enter into worship. I have seen many Churches where people spend all the time before Mass welcoming each other. This is a good thing to do if there is greeting space outside of the Church. Otherwise, silence and prayerful meditation is the most appropriate way to prepare for our encounter with Jesus both in His words and in sacrament. Please be quiet while in church. Once you enter the church – it is not the time or place to visit with those around you. If you must talk, do so as quietly and briefly as possible. Remember that your conversation might be disturbing someone who is trying to concentrate at prayer, which is much more important. This shows respect for others, for God's house and to the Lord Himself.

If for some reason, you cannot be on time, sit in the back so you do not disturb others. Do not sit on the edge of the pew if you sit down before others. Rather, sit in the middle so others do not have to climb over you. Furthermore – we should be charitable enough to offer seats to the elderly, disabled, or even suspected visitors who might be worshipping with us for the first time but who are standing.

Do not chew gum in church. It breaks your fast and it is distracting. It is generally considered impolite in a formal setting, and it does not help in any way to pray. No one chewing gum should go forward to receive communion. It is obvious that the sacred body of the Lord will end up within the gum and will eventually be discarded causing sacrilege.

When we enter and leave Church, **genuflect toward the Tabernacle.** Christ is present for our sake, and it is a sign of our faith and belief in the real and true presence of Christ in the Eucharist. By allowing our right knee to touch the floor, we acknowledge He is our Lord and God. If someone is physically unable to genuflect, then a reverent bow is sufficient. At any time, if you pass in front of the altar, the crucifix, or the tabernacle, bow reverently. Usually, a red or white light indicates that the Blessed Sacrament is reserved in the tabernacle.

Just try to remain mindful that the Church is a sacred space and place. Be conscious at all time of what is happening around you, and when you genuflect and bless yourself with holy water, say a prayer. I generally recommend the glory be to the Father or some other appropriate ejaculatory prayer.

Dress modestly and appropriately. When possible, wear your Sunday best. As Catholics, we believe that God comes down to meet us at every Mass. So, why would we not dress up? At the least, decency is required at Mass. Please dress modestly. We want to keep everyone's eyes on Jesus Christ and not be distracted by other people's inappropriate dressing.

Prepare your offering before Mass. Christ tells us not to let your left hand know what your right hand is doing when you make your offering. Keeping the basket while you get your wallet out can sometimes become quite a scene and cause unnecessary delays. In addition, if in your Church, you go up in a procession to the basket, usually placed in front of the altar, have your offering in your hands, ready so as not to hold up the line. Both at the offertory and at the thanksgiving[11], dancing - which is permissible - should be done reverently, decently and with respect for a holy place.

No bulletin reading during Mass. Imagine if you invite a guest to your house and before dinner (or during) they decide to read a magazine instead of talking to you. That is what is happening in God's house when you read the bulletin/newsletter of the parish. Always keep in mind that at every part of mass, we are lifting up our hearts, thoughts and spirit in a communion of prayers to God.

The Pastoral care of Children at Mass. Remember, your children will be the future Catholic Church goers, so let us not be so insensitive about children being children; we all must become like children to enter into the kingdom of GOD. Jesus said, "Let the children alone, and do not hinder them from coming to ME; for the kingdom of heaven belongs to such as these." (Matthew 19:14) If we do not have a children's liturgy, the children should have a section where they have people trained and assigned to look after them all through the celebration of the Holy Mass. Otherwise, parents should make sure their children are sitting with them, paying attention, and behaving. With infants, this is not easy to do. Therefore, find a 'cry room' where there is one or sit at a place where you can easily leave to pacify a crying child without causing too much commotion, which naturally becomes distraction for others.

When you are ill. If you are ill and think you may be contagious, the requirement to attend Mass is waived. You will not be committing any sin by staying away in this condition. A spiritual communion from home suffices or joining either a live streamed Mass online or on Television. Getting others sick is not charitable nor a Christian thing to do!

---

[11] A thanksgiving is popular in the African Catholic liturgy. Usually when people book masses for birthdays, anniversaries, after weddings and funerals of the elderly, they will celebrate a mass of thanksgiving specifically for the event. Usually, it is inserted into the liturgy after the post communion prayer and before the final blessing. The people celebrating will go with their family and friends in a procession, often times dancing. They will bring gifts to offer for their thanksgiving. The priest will then give them a blessing.

Participation at Mass. Be prepared and disposed for active and full participation. Join in the singing – and if your voice is not so great, make sure you are not too loud. Always remember that the choir in a Church is not there for operatic performances. When the choir wants to do something special, it is usually announced at the beginning of Mass. The sacred movements of standing, sitting, and kneeling all have their proper moments and reasons. Therefore, do your best to follow the laid-out practices of the Church. In a few instances where certain actions are physically impossible for people to carry out, remember to act in such a way that you are not awkwardly a distraction.

Hopefully your preparation for Church began before you got in your car! Remember that good Christian behavior should be exhibited on the road to and from Church and its parking lots as well! Patience is a virtue – more so because it is related to safety!

One last thing before you come in: **check that cellular phone!** Is it off or on vibrate mode? Except for people who work in essential and emergency situations, those who are on call, like doctors, nurses, fire officers, police et al, please do not leave the Church to answer calls. There is no one calling you more important than your worshipping community and God who is present in this community. The people who have these essential and life-saving jobs must also be conscious of the possibility of a call and as such find appropriate places where their leaving the Church does not constitute a distraction or disturbance for others.

Chapter Two: Participating Fully at Mass

"I will lift up the cup of salvation and call on the name of the Lord." (Ps. 116:13)

The Mass is the most important and sacred act of worship in the Catholic Church. Going to Mass is the only way a Catholic can fulfill the Third Commandment to keep holy the Sabbath day and the only regular opportunity to receive Christ in His sacred words, the assembly of His faithful people and the Holy Eucharist. The first part of the Mass in the Church is called the **Liturgy of the Word**, and its focus is on Bible readings as an integral part of daily and weekly worship. The second part is the **Liturgy of the Eucharist,** and its focus is the holiest and most sacred part of the Mass——Holy Eucharist.

The Catholic Mass incorporates hymns, gestures, symbols, prayers, sacred scriptures, sacrifice, sacred food for the soul, and directions on how to live a Christian life——all in one ceremony. The form of Catholic liturgical celebration takes its root from the early Church and celebration of the apostles. Over time, it has undergone some changes to adapt to different cultures and places. However, its fundamental structure remains the same. This same liturgy, though always a thanksgiving, can also be used for penitential purpose, for reconciliation, prayers for peace in times of disaster, civil unrest, or war. It is always a moment of grace for brothers and sisters to come together to be in communion with Christ and with each other. The beauty of Catholic worship is that anywhere in the world you may find yourself, you can go to mass, and you will always be able to celebrate meaningfully even if you do not understand a word of what is being said!

The Catholic Mass and Its Jewish Roots

As stated earlier in the introduction, many of the rituals, gestures and symbols of the Mass are drawn from Judaic ritual rites. We must keep in mind that Jesus was not a Christian! Yes, he was not. He was a faithful and Torah abiding Jew. His apostles also were temple-going Jews until after the ascension of the Lord when they were first referred to in Antioch as Christians. (cf. Acts. 11:19-26) However, we must recall that Christ's ministry was focused on a renewed knowledge of God, on how to move from the law to the spirit and how to worship God in spirit and in truth. There is no better example than the Jewish Passover and how Jesus expounded it and brought it to a newer understanding.

In this brief section, I will pay attention to the last supper and the paschal lamb. As we travel through the mass, I will refer to some connections we have with the Old Testament ritual practices of the Jews. Ideologically, the connection between the synagogue and the Church are linked in the proclamation of the word of God. In both holy places, careful attention is given to the reading and teaching of sacred scripture as a source of teaching for right and ethical living. Scripture is clear that Jesus did not only patronize the Synagogues but he went about teaching there. (cf. Mt. 6:23, 12:9; 13, Mk.1:21 etc.) At Jesus' trial, he himself told the scribes and Pharisees, "I have spoken openly to the world; I have always taught in your Synagogues and Temple" (Jn. 18:20). In the ancient texts of Justin the Martyr, titled *First Apology*, he states that the liturgy of the word evolved from the Jewish Synagogue worship. He drew out parallels, which showed clearly that the entire structure of the Catholic liturgy of the word is a direct replica of Jewish Sabbath day worship, including the prayer of the faithful, profession of faith *(shema)* and offering of gifts.

The Eucharist, as we celebrate it today, reflects both structurally and intentionally on the celebration of the Jewish Passover meal. Structurally, the Passover meal is celebrated over a series of meals, which includes roasted lamb, bitter herbs, unleavened bread and wine. Jesus, from the gospel accounts, focused on the unleavened bread and the cup of wine. These two elements will be the focal point and be at the epicenter of the new celebration of the new Passover. Intentionally, Jesus becomes the Lamb of God whose blood is shed to take away the sins of the world. Sofia Cavaletti, in her work, notes the 'dual' layer of meanings and the re-interpretation Jesus gives the Passover rite. Cavaletti states that both the Passover and last supper were both shadowed by death but were at the same time a pointer to a new life for both Israel and the apostles. Cavaletti asserts, "Jesus identified the bread with his body, so the implication was clear; just as the Lord brought forth bread from the earth so would he bring forth from the grave that body soon to be buried."[12] Further on Cavaletti expounds further that, in Jewish tradition, the unleavened bread is eaten with the lamb, "this leads to the supposition that all the prescriptions relating to the lamb were applied to the bread. Hence this would be the bread over which the Lamb of God, come to perfect the Jewish Passover sacrifice, would have pronounced the words of consecration."[13]

In entering through the mystery of Jewish memory *(shema)*, from slavery God leads His people to freedom, from death to life. In the Passover/Eucharistic meal, Jesus, the new Moses, leads God's people from slavery to sin and death to a new life. Under this veil of signs and symbols, Jesus perfected and brought into fulfilment an old rite leading to the actualization of the perfect redemption, which will be wrought by the Messiah. According to Cavaletti, "At the last supper the new words pronounced by Jesus rendered that completion present. That night the apostles could apply to one person the invocation, which had for so long expressed the yearning of the Jews: 'Blessed is He who comes in the name of the Lord.'"[14]

Central to a re-reading of the institution of the Eucharist are the words and actions of Jesus prayed over the bread and wine,

> Now as they were eating, Jesus took bread, and when he had said the blessing, he broke it and gave it to the disciples. 'Take it and eat,' he said, 'this is my body.' Then he took a cup, and when he had given thanks, he handed it to them saying, 'Drink from this, all of you, for this is my blood, the blood of the new covenant poured out for many for the forgiveness of sins. From now on, I tell you, I shall never again drink wine until the day I drink the new wine with you in the kingdom of my Father. (Mt. 26:26-29)

He took, he blessed, he broke, he gave, all replicates Jewish liturgical rituals but brought to a new understanding. For in this

---

[12] Sofia Cavaletti. "The Jewish Roots of Christian Liturgy." In Eugene J. Fisher (Ed.) The Jewish Roots of Christian Liturgy. (NY/Mahwah NJ: Paulist Press, 1990) P.23
[13] Ibid
[14] Ibid. P. 25

instance, the speaker is the one who takes, blesses, breaks, and gives Himself. It is He who then commands that this be done in memory of him, until He comes again. The Eucharist borrows from Judaic religious practices at the same time it includes newer and deeper interpretation of intentionality.

Part One: Liturgy of the Word

The celebration of mass starts with the first part, the liturgy of the word. I will try to explain its various moments, each one of which is capable of touching and involving a dimension of our humanity. It is necessary to know these holy signs to live the Mass fully and savor all its beauty.

The Procession and Entrance of the priest(s) and every available assisting minister marks the solemn beginning of the celebration of holy mass. This procession represents the entry of Christ into our gathering. This is signified in the crucifix at the head of the procession, the book of the gospels, the lighted candles symbolizing the light of Christ to all nations and all peoples. This is particularly true for the clergy present, especially in the priest who acts all through sacred liturgy in *persona Christi* – in the person of Christ, and in the people of God gathered for sacred worship. Processions for sacred rites come to us from early in the Old Testament. For instance, the book of Psalms is filled with festal processions honoring God in worship. Psalm 24 describes the tribes of Israel climbing the mountain of the Lord to God's holy temple. The Psalmist say, "Lift up your heads, O gates, rise up, your ancient portals that the king of glory may enter. (Ps. 24:9). Psalm 68:24-26, bears remarkable resemblance with Catholic liturgical procession (which may look even more like Palm Sunday) but includes every procession that leads to the altar of God. The Psalm states, "Your processions, God, are for all to see, the procession of my God, of my king, to the sanctuary; Singers ahead; musicians behind, in the middle-come girls, beating their drums. In choirs they bless God, Yahweh, since the foundation of Israel." (Ps. 68:24-25)

King David danced to the sounds of musical instruments when the Ark of the Covenant was brought up from Zion to Jerusalem (cf. 2 Sam. 6:14) And King Solomon also danced in a procession before

God. (cf. 1 Kings 8:1-10) Processions are therefore an integral part of liturgical action, it may be solemn, and it can be joyful depending on the season and the liturgy about to be celebrated.

At the foot of the altar the procession comes to a halt, traditionally a genuflection and a deep bow is observed by the priest and other extraordinary assisting ministers whose liturgical function allows them to genuflect (for instance, the cross bearer, server carrying the Thurible, deacon or lector holding the book of the gospel are not to genuflect.) In cases where the tabernacle is not reserved at the high altar or somewhere in the vicinity around the altar, a deep bow is sufficient. Here the priest and the people acknowledge the sacredness of the altar and altar space on which the grace filled sacrifice takes place. The priest then ascends to the altar much in the same way in which the psalms and the Old Testament points to going up to meet God on Sanai or in the temple.

Upon arriving at the altar, the priest **venerates** the altar. This is a significant action that not many people pay attention to. In a traditional sense, at the consecration of a Church, a relic, usually of the saint the Church is named after, is placed into the altar. The priest, on behalf of the worshipping people, reverences this relic by a kiss thereby asking the patron saint to assist the community in this action of worship. The priest arrives at the altar while the processional hymn is being sung. He goes to reverence the altar, an ancient tradition that keeps alive a Church with a memory that goes back to the beginning to acknowledge men and women who have participated before us in these sacred mysteries. In cases where mass is celebrated outside of a regular Church, veneration is not required. In cases where mass is celebrated in a Church that is not consecrated, the veneration may be performed because of the masses that have been celebrated on that altar. The veneration of the altar goes back also to the early Church when Mass was celebrated in the catacombs, mostly on the tombs of the martyrs. This is the reason for calling the stone containing the relic the *sepulcher.* Charles Belmonte points out the participation of the martyrs at mass by referencing the book of Revelation. Here John sees a vision, "I saw beneath the altar the souls of all who had been slain for love of God's word." (Rev.6:9)

In the celebration of the traditional high mass, the use of incense is required and the first incensation takes place now. The use of incense takes on many traditional meanings, scriptural and cultural. When reading the Old Testament, there are many instances where incense is used with the hope that as the incense rises, the offerings and prayers of the people will rise with it. "My prayers rise like incense, the lifting of my hands like an evening offering." (cf. Ps. 141.2) In a cultural sense, incense was used to honor dignitaries who had to make public appearances among the local people, who usually are dirty and smell. Incense, therefore, is also used to provide a fragrance that is befitting for the presence of our Eucharistic Lord. One may point out in passing that at his birth; one of the gifts from the Magi was Frankincense, which is an expensive perfume. Timothy P. O'Malley states that the incense can be seen as "*Shekinah*, the cloud of glory representative of God's very presence that descends into the holy of holies in the temple. This cloud of incense sanctifies the assembly gathered that day to participate in the Eucharistic worship of the beloved Son."[15]

Pope Francis[16] in one of his Wednesday catechesis teaches that when the priest with the other ministers reaches the altar in procession, and here he greets the altar with a bow. In a sign of veneration, kisses it and when there is incense, he incenses it. Why? Because the altar is Christ: it is a figure of Christ. When we look at the altar, we look in fact where Christ is. The Altar is Christ. These gestures, express from the beginning that the Mass is an encounter of love with Christ, who "offering His body on the cross… becomes altar, victim and priest" (Easter Preface V). In fact, the altar, in as much as sign of Christ, "is the center of the thanksgiving that is fulfilled with the Eucharist" (*Ordinamento Generale del Messale Romano*, 296), and the whole community around the altar, which is Christ: look at Christ, because Christ is at the center of the community. The altar is venerated because sacred sacrifice is offered upon them, what is offered; Christ makes the altar holy.

---

[15] Timothy P. O'Malley. *Bored Again Catholic: How the Mass Could Save Your Life*. (Huntington, Indiana: Our Sunday Visitor Publishing Division, 2017), P. 19
[16] Pope Francis used a series of his Wednesday public homilies held between January and May 2018 to discuss the Mass. I will bring his wise and fatherly teachings to support what I present. To note where I am using resources from the Holy Father, I will start with his name.

The sign of the cross -The mass traditionally starts with the symbolic self-signation with the sign of the cross upon the forehead, chest and both shoulders. This is a symbolic sign for self-blessing in the name of the Holy Trinity. From the early Church, it has been central to Catholic prayers. The sign of the cross is at the heart of the liturgy for baptism, so it remains intrinsically linked. Since baptism makes us children of God and members of His Church, it is proper that the liturgy starts with this sacred sign. It is believed that the sign of the cross sanctifies us, protects us from the power of evil and marks us for Christ (cf. Rev. &:3, 14:1) Edward Sri avers that in making the sign of the cross, we enter into a communion of sacred tradition that goes deep into the heart of sacred scripture;

> The ritual of making the sign of the cross has roots in Sacred Scripture. In particular, some Church Fathers saw the Christian practice of the sign of the cross prefigured in the Old Testament book of Ezekiel, where a mysterious mark on the forehead was used as a sign of divine protection and as a mark distinguishing the righteous from the wicked… this mark on the foreheads in Ezekiel 9 would protect the faithful ones in Jerusalem when judgement fell on the city. The New Testament saints are sealed with a similar mark. Drawing on imagery from Ezekiel, the book of Revelation depicts the saints in heaven as having a seal upon their foreheads (Rev. 7:3). As in Ezekiel's time, this seal separates the righteous people of God from the wicked and protects them from the coming judgement (Rev. 9:4)[17]

Pope Francis states, at the *sign of the cross,* the priest that presides traces it on himself and the same is done by all the members of the assembly, aware that the liturgical act is carried out "in the name of the Father and of the Son and of the Holy Spirit." The whole prayer moves, so to speak, in the realm of the Most Holy Trinity – "In the name of the Father, of the Son, and of the Holy Spirit" – which is the realm of infinite communion; it has as its origin and as its end the love of God, One and Triune, manifested and given to us in the Cross

---

[17] Edward Sri. *A Biblical Walk Through the Mass: Understanding What we Say and Do in the Liturgy.* Op.Cit. P. 20

of Christ. In fact, His Paschal Mystery is a gift of the Trinity, and the Eucharist always flows from His pierced Heart. Therefore, by signing ourselves with the sign of the cross, not only do we remember our Baptism, but also, we affirm that the liturgical prayer is the encounter with God in Christ Jesus, who became incarnate for us, died on the cross and rose glorious.

The opening greeting by the priest signifies a people enveloped in the power and presence of the Holy Trinity. Adrienne Von Speyr explains that the welcome of the priest after the sign of the cross helps the people that this holy moment depends solely in the light of Trinitarian operation and direction. Von Speyr states that "For the grace of our Lord Jesus Christ is given to us only through the self-giving love of God the Father, so that we can participate in the fellowship of the Holy Spirit."[18] Borrowing from the words of St. Paul, the priest uses one of the options provided to welcome the people; *"The grace of our Lord Jesus Christ, the Love of God and the fellowship of the Holy Spirit be with you all." (cf. 2 Cor. 13:13)*[19] Even when the priest greets the people in the shortest formula, *"The Lord be with you"*, he borrows the words of angel Gabriel in his salutation to Mary for the annunciation. He connects with the sacred greeting of angels found in several instances with the prophets and judges of the Old Testament – always at the beginning of their call to what can almost be considered 'mission impossible.' The greeting assures us like all our Biblical heroes and heroines that even in the sacred journey into the heart of scripture and sacrament, the Lord is with us. This greeting formula assures the gathered that Christ is present in His people and to His people. *"For where two or three are gathered in my name, there am I in their midst." (Mt. 18:20)* The people respond, *"And also with your spirit."* The people do not simply respond *"and also with you"*, as if it was a personal and friendly conversation. The response, *"and with your spirit"* speaks directly to the core of the priest's being, the person he is in Christ and who he represents. The call and response, praying for each other, very much characteristic of the mass starts here.

Penitential Rite – Charles Belmonte avers that the Penitential Rite comes to us from antiquity, one part that was practically part of

---

[18] Adrienne Von Speyr. *The Holy Mass.* (San Francisco: Ignatius Press,1990) P. 17

[19] Cf. also (Rom. 1:7; 1Cor. 1:3; Gal. 1:3; Eph.1:2; Phil. 1:2)

the liturgy from apostolic times. Found in the *Didache,* is found a written text, which states, "On the Lord's Day, we meet together; break the bread and give thanks, after having first confessed our sins so that our sacrifice may be pure." Then supporting this statement, Belmonte references St. Paul, "Let every man examine himself, before he eat of this bread."[20] The Liturgy of the Word is built around the penitential service and the hearing of the word of God. The priest and congregation participate in the Penitential Rite, which is simply an acknowledgment that everyone is a sinner and has sinned to some degree during the week. This **Confiteor[21],** a confessional prayer but different from the actual sacrament of penance, does not replace going to auricular confession, especially in the light of mortal sin. Rather, the Confiteor helps us to make ourselves humble before God realizing that in many ways, we fall short of the mark of our Christian calling. After a brief pause for all to recall past mistakes, the priest invites us to a public confession before God and our brothers and sisters.

> I confess to almighty God
> And to you my brothers and sisters,
> That I have greatly sinned,
> In my thoughts and in my words,
> In what I have done and in what I have failed to do.
> Through my fault, through my fault, through my most grievous fault.
> *(At this mea culpa, we strike our chest three times to mark each mea culpa, very much a sign of sorrow and regret)*
> Therefore, I ask the Blessed Virgin Mary,
> All the angels and saints
> And you, my brothers, and sisters
> To pray for me to the Lord our God.

---

[20] Charles Belmonte. *Understanding the Mass.* (Princeton, NJ: Scepter Publishers, 1989), P.55

[21] The "Confiteor" is one of the prayers that is said during the Penitential Act at the beginning of Mass of the Roman Rite in the Catholic Church. It is also said in the Lutheran Church at the beginning of the Divine Service, and by some Anglo-Catholic Anglicans before Mass. The prayer is started by the priest and joined by the people in a communal act of contrition.

Sometimes, the priest may choose to use another formula for the penitential rite, the priest brings the collective act of penitence together by praying; *"May almighty God have mercy on us, forgive us our sins, and bring us to everlasting life."* In some instances, especially when the Church is in the Easter season, it is permissible to have the blessing and sprinkling of Holy Water in place of the penitential rite and the *Kyrie* (Lord have mercy). This liturgical action recalls baptism and ritual purification from all stain of sin committed after baptism.

Followed by the **kyrie**, which expresses public guilt and shame for any sins against God and against each other, the Church begins to sum up the penitential aspect of the mass. Just like the Old Testament figures will tear their garments; we rend our hearts open to God. As they put on sack clothes, pour ashes on their heads, we also publicly acknowledge the sins of our lives even in a communal way. The priest leads the people in the tripartite call of "Lord have mercy, Christ have mercy, Lord have mercy", and we strike our hearts at each call and respond, *kyrie eleison* which translates from the Greek as "Lord Have Mercy" is taken from scripture; Bartimeaus, the blind man of Jericho, the lepers and the Canaanite woman all cried out to Jesus, Son of David (Lord, Master), have mercy/pity on me. It is this same cry of mercy, which in the liturgy the entire assembly raises in one voice to God. Before the end of the mass, at the Lamb of God, we will once again call on the mercy of the Lamb and strike our hearts in total adoration before Him.

Pope Francis teaches – that we are all sinners and, therefore, we ask for forgiveness at the beginning of the Mass. It is the *penitential act*. It is not only about thinking of the sins committed, but much more: it is the invitation to acknowledge ourselves sinners before God and before the community, before brothers and sisters, with humility and sincerity, as the publican in the Temple. If the Eucharist truly renders present the Paschal Mystery, namely the passage of Christ from death to life, then the first thing we should do is to recognize what are our situations of impending death to be able to rise with Him to new life. This makes us understand how important the penitential act is.

The Gloria, a prayer or hymn of adoration of God, addresses all three persons of the Holy Trinity. This usually sets the tone for the rest of the prayers and Bible readings at Mass. Traditionally, the priest ought to intone the Gloria while the entire congregation sings the praise of God in choir. The tone of the liturgy shifts from sorrow to a joyful song of praise, joining our voices with the angels announcing the birth of Christ to the shepherds in Bethlehem. "Glory to God in the highest, and on earth peace among men with whom he is pleased." (Lk. 2:14) Outside of Lent and Advent, the Gloria should be sung at every Sunday Mass, solemnities and feast days. Edward Sri avers "… the Gloria continues to be saturated with words from Sacred Scripture… a mosaic of biblical titles for God and common biblical expressions of praise… echoes from the Bible at every step of this prayer."[22] Sri goes further, expounding on the Gloria, "…Like a three-act play, the Gloria sums up the story of Christ's saving work moving from 1) his coming, to 2) his redeeming death, to 3) his triumphant resurrection and ascension into heaven."[23] The Gloria comes to us from the first century Church of the apostles. Every phrase of this "greater Doxology" is suffused by words taken from the epistles or biblical accounts. The Gloria is Trinitarian and echoes the song of God's reign of peace. It is the song of the Church, which has rung through the ages in praise of God. It is only right that, where it is possible, this song be accompanied by musical instrument, should be sung joyfully because it gives praise to God.

The Collect – Here the president of the assembly, the priest, invites the people to pray. "Let us pray" is the universal invocation that invites the people to join the priest at this specific prayer. From the first sign of the cross, the Church was already at prayer. It is significant to note the gesture of the priest. He opens up his arm as if to embrace the Church. Fr. Ronald Rox explains the Judaic priestly background stating, "Israel defeated the Medianites when Moses, with two friends to help him, kept his hands raised in prayer all through the battle."[24] At the prayer of the collect during mass; at the beginning of mass, the prayers over the gifts and at the conclusion of mass are carefully structured and precise. They are addressed to God as an invocation, petition is made and the conclusion which is always made through Jesus Christ, the sole mediator between

---

[22] Edward Sri. *A Biblical Walk Through The Mass: Understanding What We Do in the Liturgy.* Op.Cit. P.44
[23] Ibid. P. 46
[24] Ronald Rox. *The Mass in Slow Motion.* (England: Aeterna Press, 2014), P. 23

man and God, in the unity of the Holy Spirit. In special solemnities and feast days, reference is made appropriately to what the Church celebrates in the collect of prayers. The collect is not a verbose or long-winded charade, if it is prayed properly; it helps to focus on the central message of the readings of the day and for the mass itself. The collect is concluded by **Amen,** which we received from our Jewish antecedents. It means 'so be it' or 'be it done as you wish.' *Amen* is total submission of oneself to the will of God; a trust that God hears us. *Amen* is the last word of the scripture as found in the book of Revelation. *Amen* is the last word to all Christian faith and prayers. At this point the Church sits, ready to listen, and receive the word of God. The Church has now completed the Introit[25] and will enter into the celebration of the word of God.

Liturgy of the Word

The celebration of the liturgy of the word is essential to the celebration of the Eucharist. It has always maintained this structure from apostolic times. In the life and ministry of Jesus, teaching always came before healings, miracles or even the breaking of bread. The two disciples who encountered the risen Jesus on the road to Emmaus did not recognize him until "... starting with Moses and going through all the prophets, he explained to them the passages through the scriptures that were about himself... Now while he was with them at table, he took the bread and said the blessing; then he broke it and handed it to them. And their eyes were opened, and they recognized him..." (cf. Lk. 24:27, 30-31) The Church encounters Jesus in both word and sacrament. At the breaking of bread, our eyes are opened to see the Lord truly present in the Eucharist.

In the parochial setting, the liturgy of the word is celebrated at every mass. Every day has its own unique prayers and readings chosen by the church, not the individual parish. A Lector (one who serves in the ministry of reading sacred scripture at Mass) then reads the designated passages of the day. For regular weekday liturgy, readings that are pre-arranged in a book called the **lectionary** set

---

[25] The Introit (from Latin: introitus, "entrance") is part of the opening of the liturgical celebration of the Eucharist. In its most complete version, it consists of an antiphon psalm, the penitential rite and *Gloria Patri* sung at the beginning of the celebration. It is part of the Proper of the liturgy.

out a first reading, which is taken either from the Old Testament or from the New Testament, and then a Psalm with responses is prayed. An alleluia acclamation is proclaimed in preparation for the proclamation of the gospel. Following these readings, at the alleluia/ gospel acclamation, the congregation, which has been sitting, stands while the priest reads the Gospel, containing the very words and deeds of Christ, thus requires the respect shown by standing. For a Sunday mass, three readings are set out for the liturgy; a first reading from the Old Testament, a Psalm and response, a second reading which is usually taken from the New Testament epistles, an alleluia acclamation verse, which prepares the Church to receive the gospel.

Pope Francis teaches that in the Liturgy of the Word, which is a constitutive part because, we gather to listen to what God has done and still intends to do for us. It's an experience that happens directly and not by having heard, because when Sacred Scripture is read in Church, God Himself speaks to His people and Christ, present in the Word, proclaims the Gospel *(Ordinamento Generale del Messale Romano,* 29; Cf. Constitution *Sacrosanctum Concilium,* 7; 33)... we must listen, open our hearts, because it is God Himself who is speaking to us, and we must not think of other things or talk about other things... I will explain to you what happens in this Liturgy of the Word. The pages of the Bible cease to be a writing to become living word pronounced by God. It is God, who through the person that reads, speaks to us and questions us who listen with faith. The Spirit "who has spoken through the prophets" (Creed) and has inspired the sacred authors, acts so "that the Word of God truly operates in hearts what He makes resound in ears" *(Lectionary,* Introd., 9). However, to listen to the Word of God it is necessary to have an open heart to receive the word in the heart. God speaks and we listen to Him, to then put into practice what we have heard. It is very important to listen. Sometimes, perhaps, we do not understand well because there are some readings that are a bit difficult. However, God speaks the same to us in another way. [It is necessary to be] in silence and to listen to the Word of God.

We need to listen to Him! It is, in fact, a question of life, as the incisive expression well reminds that "man shall not live by bread alone, but by every word that proceeds from the mouth of God" *(Matthew* 4:4) — the life that the Word of God gives us. In this connection, we speak of the Liturgy of the Word as the "table" that the Lord prepares to feed our spiritual life. That of the Liturgy is an abundant table, which draws widely from the treasures of the Bible (Cf. *SC,* 51) be it of the Old or of the New Testament, because, in them, the Church, proclaims the one and the same mystery of Christ (Cf. *Lectionary,* Introd., 5). The Holy Father states that we think of the richness of the biblical Readings offered by the three Sunday cycles, in the light of the Synoptic Gospels, accompanying us in the course of the Liturgical Year: a great richness. I wish to recall here the importance of the Responsorial Psalm, whose function is to foster meditation on all that was heard in the Reading that preceded it. It is good that the Psalm is enhanced with the song, at least in the refrain (Cf. *OGMR,* 61; *Lectionary,* Introd., 19-22).

The liturgical proclamation of the same Readings, with the songs deduced from Sacred Scripture, expresses, and fosters ecclesial communion, accompanying the path of each and all. One understands, therefore, why liturgical laws prohibit subjective choices, such as the omission of Readings or their substitution with non-biblical texts. I have heard that some, if there is news, read the newspaper, because it is the news of the day. No! The Word of God is the Word of God! We can read the newspaper later, but there, the Word of God is read. It is the Lord who speaks to us. To substitute that Word with other things, impoverishes and compromises the dialogue between God and His people in prayer. On the contrary, [required is] the dignity of the pulpit and the use of the Lectionary, the availability of good readers and psalmists. However, it is necessary to find good readers! – those who can read, not those who read [mangling the words] and nothing is understood. It is so – good readers are needed. They must prepare themselves and try before the Mass to read well. And this creates a receptive atmosphere of silence.

We know that the Lord's word is an indispensable aid not to get lost, as the Psalmist well recognizes that, addressing the Lord, confesses: "Thy word is a lamp for my feet and a light to my path" (*Psalm* 119:105). How can we face our earthly pilgrimage, with its toils and trials, without being regularly fed and illumined by the Word of God that resounds in the Liturgy? It is certainly not enough to listen with the ears, without receiving in the heart the seed of the divine Word, enabling it to bear fruit. Let us remember the parable of the sower and the different results according to the different types of soil (Cf. *Mark* 4:14-20). The action of the Spirit, which renders the response effective, is in need of hearts that allow themselves to be worked and cultivated, so that what is heard at Mass passes in daily life. In keeping with the Apostle James' admonition: "Be doers of the word, and not hearers only, deceiving yourselves" (*James* 1:22). The Word of God makes a path within us. We hear it with our ears, and it passes to the heart. It does not stay in the ears; it must go to the heart and from the heart, it passes to the hands, to good works. The Word of God follows this course: from the ears to the heart to the hands. Let us learn these things. Criteria and ordering of the Readings of the Mass in the Roman Rite are described in the *Introduction* to the *Lectionary.* "The Liturgy of the Word must be celebrated in a way to foster meditation. Therefore, all forms of haste that impede recollection must be avoided. Opportune in it also are brief moments of silence, adapted to the gathered assembly, through which, with the help of the Holy Spirit, the Word of God is heard in the heart and the response is prepared with prayer" *(OGMR, 56)*.

The First Reading

In the celebration of the Mass during ordinary times, the first reading is usually from the Old Testament. At some specific seasons and solemnities, especially at Easter when we read from the Acts of the Apostles, it is possible to use a first reading from the New Testament. The way, in which the lectionary has been pre-arranged, the first reading always provides a foundation for the gospel. The liturgy is built around the prophetic promises found in the Old Testament and their fulfilment in the New Testament. Sometimes these overlapping readings provide grounds for continuity or contrast, but they always provide the grounds for a better understanding of Jesus. The congregation sits through the first and second readings. It reflects on the instances where people sit out in the outskirts of towns, out in the fields, in Mary, Martha and Lazarus' home, at the feet of the Lord to listen to His words. At the end of the first reading, the reader tells the assembly, "The word of the Lord." Because that exactly is what it is, the word of God. In gratitude, the people respond, "Thanks be to God." Preparations for where the word will be proclaimed from (and when necessary, making available an effective microphone system) is the responsibility of the deacon or priest while the proper proclamation of the word is entrusted to the trained lector.

The Responsorial Psalm

Traditionally, for most liturgies, the vesicle of psalms from the Old Testament is used with a response after each stanza. Again, the psalms belong to Judaism and the way in which we sing it comes to us from the apostles who in turn carried on the singing of psalms from their Judaic traditions. Monastic life celebrates the psalms and so do priests and men and women religious. The psalms express various aspects of God's holiness, kindness, and omnipotence; it provides a place of refuge for us on our pilgrim journey. The spiritual riches of the psalms cannot be over emphasized. The writer Paula Houston referencing Dom Paul Delatte says of the psalms, "The psalter was created by God Himself to be forever the authentic formulary of prayer. With its thoughts and in its language, God has willed to be praised and honored. The psalms express the deepest, most varied, and most delicate sentiments of the human heart, and answer all its needs. They served the saints of the Old Testament; they have served the Apostles and the saints of all ages… They were said and said again by Our Lady and Our Lord."[26] All are encouraged to sing joyfully the response while the cantor leads by singing the verses. St. Paul teaches that, "Let the words of Christ, in all its richness, find a home with you. Teach each other, and advise each other, in all wisdom. With gratitude in your hearts sing psalms and hymns and inspired songs to God…" (cf. Col. 3:16)

The Second Reading

This reading always comes from the New Testament books, mostly the Epistles, Acts of the Apostles, or the book of Revelation. Mostly, these readings are exhortational and may not necessarily reflect either the first or gospel reading. They draw from the mystery of the life, ministry, suffering and death of Jesus to challenge the Christian and the Church to holiness of life. Wuerl and Aquilina in their work makes the link, "From the second reading we come to know that our fellowship is not just with Christians in our parish,

---

26   Paula Huston. One Ordinary Sunday: A Meditation on the Mystery of the Mass. (Notre Dame, Indiana: Ave Maria Press, 2016), P.48

in our time. It is *catholic* – that is, universal. It embraces all the people of the world, at every period of the Church's history. We are still living in the Church described in the apostle's letters. We want to be faithful, as that first generation was…"[27] Since these epistles (letters) where catechesis and instructional for the first Christian faith communities, they remain the same for us today.

The Alleluia Verse/Gospel Acclamation

The Alleluia liturgically is supposed to be sung at all times except during lent when it is excluded from the rite of celebration. Alleluia is a Hebrew word, which literally translates as "Praise Yahweh" or "Praise the Lord." It is found often in the psalms (known also in Hebrew as *Hallel*) and plays a pivotal part in the Jewish celebration of the Passover. The reason for the celebration of the Passover, from which Jesus established the Eucharist, is intrinsically linked to salvation. This in itself is a gift that comes from God; therefore, to "praise the Lord" is right. The Alleluia also predisposes the people to receive the Gospel where Jesus will speak directly to His people. The same Alleluia is the song of the angels in Revelation 19 where, in John's vision, he sees a multitude in a festival of praise,

> After this, I heard what seemed to be the great sound of a huge crowd in heaven, singing, Alleluia! Salvation and glory and power to our God! … Then the twenty four elders and the four living creatures threw themselves down and worshipped God seated on his throne, and they cried, "Amen, Alleluia…" Then a voice came from the throne; it said 'Praise our God, you servants of his, those who fear him, small and great alike. And I heard what seemed to be the voices of a huge crowd, like the sound of the ocean, or the great roar of thunder, answering, Alleluia! The reign of the Lord our God almighty has begun; let us be glad and joyful and give glory to God, for this is the time for the marriage of the Lamb. (cf. Rev. 19:1, 4-8)

---

[27] Cardinal Donald Wuerl & Mike Aquilina. The Mass: The Glory, The Mystery, The Tradition. (New York: Image Random House Publishing, 2011), P. 117

It is customary to stand once the Alleluia verse is raised, and in some masses, there is a procession with lighted candles and the book of the gospel from its place of honor on the altar or in a designated and befitting area. In the case of a high Mass, the *thurible* accompanies the procession. This indicates that the gospel is truly a light to our feet and on our path. (cf. Ps. 119:105) We stand because, just as Christ is present in the sacred species of bread and wine, so is he also present in His word. This is why the book of the gospels should occupy a place of honor within the liturgy and even in our homes. It is for the same reason that we venerate the holy book, and the appropriate minister to proclaim the gospel will incense it and kiss it. Within the singing of the first Alleluia, a verse of scripture is sung or read. It helps us to focus on the theme of the day based on the reading for the day. After this, the Alleluia verse is repeated, and the Church is ready to receive the gospel.

The Gospel Reading

If a deacon is to proclaim the gospel, he must first ask for a blessing from the presider (either a bishop or a priest). He will go to the presider and bowing will say, *"Father, give me your blessing that I may worthily proclaim the gospel."* The presider responds while blessing the deacon, *"May the Lord be upon your heart and your lips that you may worthily proclaim His good news."* If a priest is to proclaim the gospel, he goes to the front of the altar, the crucifix or where the book of the gospel is placed, and bowing deeply, he asks the Lord, *"May the Lord be upon my heart and my lips that I may worthily proclaim your good news."* These prayers are said because the ministers must always keep in mind that they do nothing of themselves both in the proclamation and the teaching that follows; it is Christ who enables the minister to act in His person. He will simultaneously bless himself with the sign of the cross. He picks up the book of the gospel and processes to the *ambo* from where the gospel traditionally is proclaimed.

The minister (priest or deacon) who proclaims the gospel first invites the people with the words; *"The Lord be with you"* – a reminder of whose presence they are and who is about to speak to them; the Lord Himself. The people respond as usual, *"And with your spirit."* He then introduces the gospel; *"A reading from the Holy gospel according to..."* He traces the sign of the cross on the face of the book of the gospel and with the people also make the sign of the cross on his forehead, on his lips and on his chest. In this gesture, the entire Church asks the Lord to open our minds to receive His word, to open our lips to proclaim the message we receive and to let this same word live in our hearts. The gospel is listened to as one listens to someone else speak to him or her. All must be standing in the age-old tradition in honor of the gospel, and when it is concluded, the minister lets us know by holding the book up for all to see and says, *"The gospel of the Lord."* To which in gratitude the entire Church responds, *"Praise be to you Lord Jesus Christ."* Until the 13th Century, the book of the gospel was brought to be kissed by the celebrant. Now, only when a deacon proclaims the gospel, and the bishop is present is the book brought to be kissed by the bishop. When proclaimed by a priest, he kisses the book of the gospel in veneration on behalf of the people gathered for that liturgy. The proclaimer prays though inaudibly on behalf of everyone, *"May the words of the holy gospel wipe away our sins."*

The Homily -The congregation sits and listens to the homily, which in Greek means explanation. It is a reflection on the Word of God given only by an ordained clergy member, deacon or priest only in the Catholic Church. The priest connects the Scripture readings to the daily lives of the people, the teachings of the Church, or the particular celebration at hand. On Sundays and all other holy days, the homily should not be omitted, rather it should be an occasion to expound on the mysteries of Christ in His Church and how the good news impact daily living. Alfred McBride, while explaining the importance of the homily, states,

> Preaching and explaining God's word has been a source of faith growth since New Testament times. St. Paul gives us and the homilist the clearest reason for preaching: "How can they call on him in whom they have not believed? And how can they believe in him of whom they have not heard? And how can they hear without someone to preach? As it is written, 'How

beautiful are the feet of those who bring good news!'
(cf. Rom. 10:14-15)[28]

The Holy Father, Pope Francis in one of his Wednesday catechesis underscores the importance of the moment of teaching through the homily. His teaching is worth noting carefully.

Pope Francis: The Holy Father reflecting on homilies instructs that to bring His message, Christ also makes use of the word of the priest who, after the Gospel, gives the homily. Earnestly recommended by Vatican Council II as part of the liturgy itself, the homily is not a circumstantial discourse or a catechesis, such as the one I am giving now –, or a conference or not even a lesson; the homily is something else. What is the homily? It is "a taking up again of the dialogue already open between the Lord and His people, so that it finds fulfilment in life. The Gospel's authentic exegesis is our holy life! The Lord's word ends its course becoming flesh in us, translated into works, as happened with Mary and the Saints. Remember what I said the last time, the Word of the Lord enters by the ears, reaches the heart, and goes to the hands, to good works. And the homily also follows the Lord's Word and follows this course as well to help us, so that the Lord's Word, passing through the heart, reaches the hands.

One who gives the homily must fulfil well his ministry – he, who preaches, the priest, or the deacon or the Bishop – offers a real service to all those taking part in the Mass, but those who hear him must also do their part. First of all, by paying due attention, namely, by assuming the right interior dispositions, without subjective demands, knowing that every preacher has merits and limitations. If sometimes there is reason to be bored by a long, or unfocused, or incomprehensible homily, at other times, instead, it is prejudice that is the obstacle. The one who gives a homily must be conscious that he is not doing something of his own; he is preaching, giving voice to Jesus, he is preaching the Word of Jesus. The homily must be well prepared; it must be brief, brief! "Brief," "brief," "not more than ten minutes, stressed Pope Francis regarding the "service' that the homily constitutes, so that the Word of God, heard during the

---

[28]Alfred McBride, O.Praem. *Celebrating the Mass: A Guide for Understanding and Loving the Mass More Deeply.* (Huntington, Indiana: Our Sunday Visitor Publishing Division, 1999), P. 29

liturgy, passes from the ear to the heart and to the hands and makes one act in keeping with the Gospel. And how often we see that during the homily some fall asleep, others chat or go outside to smoke a cigarette . . . Therefore, please, make the homily brief, but it must be well prepared. And how is a homily prepared, dear priests, deacons, and Bishops? How is it prepared? With prayer, with the study of the Word of God and by doing a clear and brief synthesis; it must not go beyond ten minutes.[29]

By way of conclusion, we can say that, through the Gospel and the Homily, in the Liturgy of the Word, God dialogues with His people, who listen to Him with attention and veneration and, at the same time, recognize Him present and operating. If then, we listen to the "Good News," we will be converted and transformed by it, therefore we will be capable of changing the world and ourselves. Why? Because the "Good News,"- the Word of God enters the ears, goes to the heart, and reaches the hands to do good works. However, for this to be the case a well-disposed assembly is necessary, which is prepared by familiarity with the Word of God. Therefore, after the homily, **a time of silence enables one to settle the seed received in the spirit, so that resolutions of adherence are born to what the Spirit has suggested to each one.** Silence after the homily — there must be a beautiful silence there — and each one must think about what he or she has heard. *Note: In many Churches, especially major cities with huge congregations, there is the tendency to jump right away into the creed without any time to reflect and listen to God in the depths of our hearts.*

On Sundays and holy days, the homily is followed by the **Profession of Faith, or Creed**, which succinctly sums up all the fundamental doctrinal teachings of the Church, which is said or sung. The creed,

---

[29] The advocacy for a 10-minute homily at the maximum by the Holy Father, I believe speaks to the Churches of the Western hemisphere. In the global South, no matter how concise and sound the priest's homily might be, especially for a Sunday liturgy, it is culturally unacceptable for the homily to be 10 minutes short! Most cultures will dwell on the use of short stories, proverbs, and songs to elucidate and draw out the meaning of the message of the day within the context of the word of God proclaimed for that Sunday. An average homily for a Sunday Mass will be 20 minutes at the shortest and I have seen longer ones between 45 minutes to an hour. Are there abuses? Certainly! However, when the people encounter a priest who is gifted in the art of preaching, they are not worried about leaving the Church early.

from the Latin, *Credo* means 'I believe.' It is a summary statement of the Christian Faith as it has been in use from the early Church. It is also a measuring rod against wrong doctrine and the curbing of heresy. It is biblical because it goes through the history of salvation; from the book of Genesis to the book of Revelation espousing the Christian belief in creation, fall, virgin conception of the incarnate word, redemption, and the trinity. Edward Sri states, "We must see the creed we recite at Mass as our Shema. Like the Shema of old, our creed has a counter-cultural message today. It tells a different story about life than what is commonly taught in the modern, secular world. Ours is an era of relativism –the view that there is no moral or religious truth, no right or wrong."[30] Sri continues that this relativistic worldview claims that life has no meaning; as such, people are free to do whatever it is they want with their lives. We pray the creed, either recited or sung, at every major celebration of the Mass. Like the Mass itself, the constancy with which we repeat these actions and words so we can become more entrenched in the words and their meaning. One who eats three meals everyday does not become tired of the frequency, since it is needed for nutrition and wellbeing. Also, like those who are in love, they never tire to want to be with each other, hold hands, take long walks and say 'I love you' to each other. Between the Apostles' Creed and the Nicene (325)/ Chalcedonian (451) creed, the Church celebrates the living faith in Jesus as given to the Apostles who faithfully passed it on to us. The creed is used in the profession of faith at baptism and at the reception of an adult into the Catholic Church and at confirmation. In some religious congregations, to take the final vows requires the recitation of the creed. Whenever a cleric assumes a new pastorate and is to be officially installed, or when a bishop is to be consecrated, or when a cardinal is to be created, the creed is said in a personal profession of faith. For Catholics who live in secular societies, or poly-religious cultures, praying the creed regularly and meditating on each article of faith is a sure support against heresy and contamination of fabricated doctrines. The creed is said to stand within a communal act of worship like the Mass. In some private settings, like taking of religious vows, the candidate may kneel according to the culture or discipline of the place.

---

[30] Edward Sri. *A Biblical Walk Through the Mass*... Op.Cit. Pp.72-2

Then comes the **Prayers of the Faithful**, which are petitions that are offered by the people of God gathered for worship for the pope, the Church, the civil authorities, current concerns, and so on, to which the people respond to the invitation by the leader, *"We pray to the Lord,"* -- *"Lord, hear our prayer"* or *"Hear us, O Lord."* The entire Mass as the sacrifice of Christ is a thanksgiving and all of it is prayers. The petitions spoken of here are specific to some particular intentions, which are always prepared before the liturgy and should bear direct link to the liturgy of the day. It may also include some current societal issues affecting people like natural disasters, war, epidemic, etc. The Church also responds to St. Paul's teaching; "First of all, I ask that supplications, prayers, petitions, and thanksgiving be offered for everyone, for kings and for all in authority, that we may lead a quiet and tranquil life in all devotion and dignity. This is good and pleasing to God our savior." (1Tim.2:1-3) Under liturgical norms, the bidding prayers should not be left open to anyone who is "moved by the Spirit" to pray spontaneously without order and a specific theme. They ought to be precise and to the point. The response can be sung or said. Care must be taken that it does not degenerate into verbose, long-winded diatribe aimed at showing off of scripture quotes, passing on information, or unnecessarily wasting time and dragging the mass on and on. The prayer of the faithful signals the end of the first part of the liturgy, the liturgy of the word gives way to the Eucharist – from word to sacrament; from been fed with the word of God to been fed with the body of Christ.

Chapter Three: Part II: Liturgy of the Eucharist

Pray brothers and Sisters that my sacrifice and yours will be made acceptable to God, our almighty father. (Canon of the Mass)

The liturgy moves on to **the Offertory,** the material gifts are taken up in a collection at this time. In some parts of the world, this is just money. In some other cultures, it may include agricultural products, food, and animals. They are usually donated to support missionary priests and to support the expenses of the local Church. (There are other specified Sundays for collections, which are taken as support for other things outside of the parish.) This tradition can be found in the writings of St. Justin Martyr (AD 115) and St. Hippolytus (AD 225) which attests that this practice was common in the early Church. People brought wool, honey, bread, oil, wax, etc., as part of the offertory. A collection was also taken which was used to cater for widows, orphans, strangers and the poor. The offertory from the Latin word *Offere*, meaning to present or bring forth, is a ritual where all the gifts for the poor are brought forward by designated people with bread, wine and water. They emphasize the character of the crucified one who on the cross when pierced on the side, had water and blood gush forth. On the people's part, they symbolically represent our little efforts to bring something forward for the sacrifice of which Christ Himself is priest and victim. Note that there is yet another procession here. In climes where a basket is passed around at the collections or people go to the foot of the altar and offer their gifts there personally, this is a joyful part of the liturgy, which should be celebrated appropriately with music and joy.

The presentation of bread and wine symbolizes not only the offering back to God of the people gathered but also the work, joys and sorrows of God's people. Symbolically, whatever we offer comes first from Him. This is why in the prayers during Mass; we acknowledge that bread and wine are fruit of the earth and work of human hands. Belmonte states it thus,

> The little piece of bread on the paten represents, poetically, the union of man's work with the earth, a natural element... when we offer bread as a participation in Christ's sacrifice, we intend to offer

49

also all the beauty and goodness of nature united to our own work... we recall the gospel episode of the multiplication of the loaves and the fish. Here in the Mass, Christ is going to feed, with the food of immortality, all who are willing to accept him. But as in the gospel scene, he wants us to put in whatever we have.[31]

Giving of money also, carries the sentiments that hours of work by which we earn our keep are brought back humbly to God. This ritual action teaches us to remember that all things come from God; we ought to give from the gifts He has given us, only then are we blessed more in return.

Preparation of Gifts

The priest or deacon, having received the gifts presented by the people, brings the chalice, ciborium, wine, and water to the altar. If the basket for the monetary collection is presented with the gifts, it is placed at the foot of the altar. A corporal is always placed on the altar before the chalice and ciborium are placed on the altar. A corporal is a white piece of cloth; its sole purpose is to preserve particles from the sacred host from irreverently falling to the ground and not to constitute a sacrilege. The priest then lifts the paten containing the large host[32] and prays; *"Blessed are you Lord God of all creation, for through your goodness we have received this bread which we offer you, fruit of the earth and work of human hands, it will become for us the bread of life."* The people respond, *"Blessed be God forever."* The priest, in preparation for the blessing of the wine, first will do the co-mingling. He will pour the wine into the chalice and add a drop of water, while saying quietly, *"By the mystery of this water and wine may we come to share in the divinity of Christ, who humbled himself to share in our humanity."* Edward Sri notes that in the co-mingling there is a profound theological significance; the wine symbolizes

---

[31] Charles Belmonte. *Understanding the Mass.* Op. Cit. P 113

[32] The piece of unleavened white bread used for the Eucharist is known as host from the Latin *'hostire'* meaning to strike, which reflects on an animal about to be struck down for sacrifice. According to scholars, among the oriental world, "it is called 'the lamb' and also, 'the seal.' For it carried a sign or mark. On the other hand, the consecrated host is called 'the first born' and 'the blazing coal.' (cf. Charles Belmonte. *Understanding the Mass.* Op.Cit. P. 112

Christ's divinity and water symbolizes humanity. The mingling of wine and water, therefore, points us to the mystery of the incarnation, and the invitation to partake in the divine nature.[33] In his reflections on the mass, Ronald Knox avers that the co-mingling of water and wine reminds us of becoming one with Christ, "our identity merged and lost in his, just as the identity of that spot of water is merged and lost in the wine that covers the bottom of the chalice."[34] He states further that the entire point of the offertory is to remind us how little it is we offer, so that at the consecration we may bow humbly, more than ever, by the thought of what he makes of it.

Some other scholars see in the co-mingling a symbol of the mystery of the union between Christ and His Church, some others still as a vivid image of the blood and water that came from the pierced side of Christ on the cross. (cf. Jn.19:34) Most of all, the drop of water is absolved into the wine which after consecration becomes the blood of Christ. It is in this same way, we are absorbed into Christ, as we become what we consume. The blessing invoked by the priest over bread and wine is traced back to Jewish Sabbath practices, an ancient prayer known as *Kiddush*, still in practice today among the Jews, the prayer always starts out as "Blessed be God..."[35] Timothy O'Malley sees another link to ancient Jewish prayer patterns, and states,

> This style of prayer, performed over the Eucharistic elements of bread and wine, is an old one. It is called *Berakah* (Blessing) prayer. Israel used to thank God for everything in this fashion. During morning prayers, Israel would pray: 'You are blessed, Lord our God, king of the universe, you who form the light and create the darkness (Is.45:7); who shed the light of your mercy upon the earth and those who dwell on it; who, out of goodness constantly renew every day the works of your creation.[36]

---

[33] Edward Sri. *A Biblical Walk Through the Mass...* Op.Cit. P. 89

[34] Ronald Knox. *The Mass in Slow Motion.* (New York: Aeterna Press, 2014), P.38

[35] Paula Huston. *One Ordinary Sunday: A Meditation on the Mystery of the Mass.* Op.Cit. P. 129

[36] Timothy P. O'Malley. *Bored Again Catholic...* Op. Cit. P. 117

The blessings over bread and wine are essential to the preparation of the gifts because of its ancient roots. Archeological materials going as far back as the first millennium show that the same blessing over bread and wine were used at the Passover meal. Meaning that they are also the words Jesus applied to the first Eucharist.[37]

After the co-mingling, the priest lifts up the chalice and repeats the blessing over the cup, *"Blessed are you Lord God of all creation for through your goodness we have received the wine we offer you, fruit of the vine and work of human hand; it will become our spiritual drink."* Again, the people respond, *"Blessed be God forever."* At the elevation of both bread and wine, we are beginning to be pointed in the direction in which our sacrifice and our whole being will be directed. As the priest stands at the altar, the Church recalls the priests of old who stood at various altars blessing God on behalf of the people. One easily recalls Melchizedek, the first priest of sacred scripture, who while offering bread and wine also prayed, "Blessed be Abram by God the highest." (Gen. 14:19-20) The priest places the chalice back on the corporal, takes a deep bow and prays quietly, *"Lord be pleased to accept this sacrifice offered with a humble and contrite heart."* This recalls Daniel and his three companions, Shedrach, Meshach and Abednego while in the furnace, they petitioned Yahweh with a humble and contrite heart that they may be made acceptable like burnt offerings found in the Temple. (Dn. 3:39-40) At this point, the priest moving slightly to one side of the altar, ritually washes his hands (known as *lavabo*) while praying in the words of David in Psalm 51:2, *"Lord wash away my iniquities and cleanse me of all my sins."* It signifies the ritual cleansing observed by Jews in preparation for prayers (also known as *ablution.*) Here, just like the Levitical priests of old, the priest is getting ready to enter the 'holy of holies.' It recalls baptism and the washing away of sins, and the priest's personal desire for interior purity, acknowledging his own human frailty, he asks God for help so he can worthily offer the sacrament of thanksgiving.

With arms outstretched in the *orans* position, he invites the people to unity, using in some way, a longer version of "Let us Pray," the priest says, *"Pray brothers and sisters (brethren) that my sacrifice and yours may be made acceptable to God our father the Almighty."*

[37] Donald Wuerl & Mike Aquilina. *The Mass...* Op.Cit. P. 143-4

Edward Sri takes note of 'my' and 'yours' – establishing the sacred character of this sacrifice in which Christ's sacrifice will be made present through the instrumentality of the priest acting *In Persona Christi* – in the person of Christ. And the 'Your' part refers to the entire Church offering the mass in union with Christ. The people respond, *"May the Lord accept the sacrifice at your hands for the praise and glory of his name for our good and the good of all his holy Church."* Again, an acknowledgement that the sacrifice belongs to Christ and that we have a share in its divine merits. The priest then offers the prayer over the gifts. All stand as we sum up the preparation of the gifts and prepare for the preface. Charles Belmonte shares his thoughts on the prayer over the gifts which I think better reflects on the entire preparation of gifts,

> In prayer over the gifts, we usually acknowledge our incapacity to offer to God gifts adequate to His goodness and power. We ask God to accept what we offer with sincerity. We ask for some grace in connection with the mystery celebrated on that particular day, in return for the material gifts. We notice an ascending or upward striving rhythm in the progress of the liturgical action. If we contrast this prayer with the collect, we can perceive an increase in fervor and assurance. We know that our gifts to God will be returned to us multiplied a hundredfold.[38]

This brings the celebration to the **PREFACE,** the prayer that prepares us to encounter Jesus in the Eucharistic prayers. The preface reflects on the seasons or celebrations of the Church's life. Every preface reflects on the greatness of God in the incarnation, ministry, death, resurrection, ascension, and the redemptive action it achieved. The preface plays an important role in getting our minds individually and collectively situated for the most sacred prayers the Church is about to enter into. Since the Eucharist itself is a thanksgiving, the preface, which is filled with thanks and praise of God, is most appropriate. The prefaces usually have similar beginning with the call and response between the priest and the people of God.

---

[38] Charles Belmonte. *Understanding the Mass. Op.Cit.* P. 116

Priest: *The Lord be with you (This invitation to prayer has been discussed earlier.)*

People: *And with your spirit (Same here)*

Priest: *Lift up your hearts (The Priest invites the people to focus on heaven)*

People: *We lift them up to the Lord (The people acknowledge that it is necessary to lift our hearts up, but up to the Lord.)*[39]

Priest: *Let us give thanks to the Lord our God.*

People: *It is right and just.*

Priest: *Father all powerful and ever living God, we do well always and everywhere to give you thanks,*[40] *through Jesus Christ our Lord*

Adrienne Von Speyr explains the work of the preface in very articulate terms thus,

> The preface… provides the transition to the Canon. It is a final purification of priest and congregation, an act of gratitude to God and confession of his divinity. This confession is like an echo of the confession of sin. But whereas the Confiteor is a confession of personal sin, what is here confessed is the magnificence of God. After the confession, our freedom from sin facilitates the transition into pure praise of God, freed from any residual self-interest or self-perfection. Each preface, for every feast and season in the Church's year, flow into the single, unchanging *Sanctus.*[41]

---

[39] This lifting up of the heart *(Sursum Corda)* reflects on the teachings of St. Paul in Col.3:1-2), "If then you have been raised with Christ, seek the things that are above, where Christ, is seated at the right hand of God. **Set your minds on things that are above,** not on things that are on earth."

[40] There are various Pauline texts that teaches the importance of giving thanks; "Abound in thanksgiving" (Col.2:7), Giving thanks to God in all we do and always, in all circumstances. (Cols. 3:17, 1 Thess. 5:18, Phil. 4:6, 1 Cor. 14:16-19, Eph. 5:19-20)

[41] Adrienne Von Speyr. *The Holy Mass.* Op.Cit. Pp.55-6

The **Sanctus** takes the pattern of the tripartite invocation, adoration, and worship of God. From the beginning of mass, we have seen many forms of prayers and invocation which follows the thrice pattern of call and response prayers. The Holy, Holy, Holy is a confession of God's greatness and holiness which we are invited into at the Eucharistic prayer. The Church universal sings this song with one voice and one accord,

> *Holy, Holy, Holy Lord God of Hosts*
> *Heaven and earth are full of your glory.*
> *Hosanna in the highest.*
> *Blessed is he who comes in the name of the Lord.*
> *Hosanna in the highest.*

Sanctus, from Latin, means Holy, (In the Eastern rite Churches, it is called the Trisagion) recalls a vision of Prophet Isaiah. Here the Prophet sees "… the Lord sitting upon a throne, high and lifted up; and His train filled the temple, above stood the seraphim; each one had six wings; with two wings they covered their faces, and with two they covered their feet, and with two they were flying. And one cried unto the other, and said, Holy, Holy, Holy, is the Lord almighty; the whole earth is full of your glory." (Is. 6:1-3) According to Edward Sri, the three-fold repetition of the word 'Holy' is the strongest form of the superlative in the Hebrew language. Therefore, the seraphim worshipping God as all holy "acclaim the Lord as all holy one, the one God above all other gods. And by singing 'the earth is full of your glory,' they praise God for His splendor, which is displayed throughout creation."[42]

We find a corollary in John's visions in the Book of Revelation where he encounters a heavenly liturgy, where John sees the 'son of man' radiant in glory. In fear, John falls before Jesus – 'the son of man.' Like the Prophet Isaiah, John sees the winged seraphim who sing the hymn of praise to God, "Holy, Holy, Holy is the Lord God Almighty, who was and who is and who is to come." (Rev. 4:8) In John's vision, there were twenty-four elders who fall down before God's throne singing hymns of praise to God, "Worthy are you, our Lord and God, to receive glory and honor and power, for you created all things and by your will were they created and have their being."

---

[42] Edward Sri. *A Biblical Walk Through the Mass...* Op.Cit. P. 103

(Rev. 4:11) The angels, the twenty-four elders who sit on twenty-four thrones in heaven, Isaiah and John, all fall prostrate before the majesty of God. This is the same reason, as we conclude the *Sanctus;* we fall on our knees in the presence of His divine majesty. The concluding part to the Sanctus, "Hosanna is He who comes" should remind us of Christ's triumphant entry into Jerusalem. It evokes our preparation to receive Him as the Messiah. It also reminds us that the same crowd shouting Hosanna will soon be the same crowd to cry, "Crucify him, crucify him."

The elements that are central and uniform all through the various Eucharistic prayers are: the praise of God, thanksgiving, the invocation of the Holy Spirit over the gifts at consecration (also known as *Epiclesis)*, then the Anamnesis –the memorial- *"do this in memory of me."* The Church offers up Christ our oblation to the Father through the Holy Spirit. Then the Church intercedes in prayers for the living and the dead. At the *per ipsum* – this is the exclamation that signifies the end of the Eucharistic prayer. The Church prays the doxology of the Eucharistic Prayer. The entire Eucharistic prayer is said by the priest or with con-celebrating priests only. At this point, mostly, through his actions and words, lifting up his hands, opening them in prayer, stretching them over the gifts, praying the words of the *anaphora,* blessing the gift with the sign of the cross, lifting up the chalice and the pattern, he, the priest, is truly acting *In persona Christi.*

Timothy O'Malley makes a very important point that we must always hold in our minds as we approach this most sacred moment of the Mass. The bread and wine point us to the paschal sacrifice. This is made more deeply manifest by the priest's first blessing with the sign of the cross on the gifts. The Eucharist may seem repetitious as some people complain, yet it is in this repetitiveness that lies the very heart of what makes the Church 'catholic' and 'Apostolic.' It is truly and indeed our connection to Jesus and the apostles in the upper room. O'Malley warns that while the mass recalls the sacrifice of Christ on the cross, it is not 'killing' Christ repeatedly. Christ's sacrifice is once and for all. The holy Mass is purely a sacramental memorial of Christ's death and His resurrection. O'Malley states, "Sacrifice, for the Church, is not fundamentally about pain. It is not fundamentally about suffering. Rather, sacrifice is love. At every

Mass, we participate in the sacrifice of God's love."[43] This point cannot be over emphasized for miracle seekers and Church voyeurists; the Mass is the greatest miracle right in front of our eyes. It is about life overcoming death, the resurrection overcoming suffering. At the celebration of Mass and at the exposition of the Blessed Sacrament, we must learn to bring our suffering, hopes and aspirations to the Eucharistic Lord. O'Malley sums up the actions of sacrifice based on love by saying, "the language of sacrifice in the Roman Canon reminds us that the Mass is sacrifice of love. The more we receive this sacrifice, the more we offer this sacrifice of love ourselves, the more we can become God's love for the world. Total love is given in the Eucharist. Total love is received in the Eucharist."[44]

After the preface, the Roman Canon for the Latin rite is prayed – also known from the Greek as *Anaphora*. Originating in Rome from around the fourth century but was developed during the papacy of Pope St. Gregory the Great around the 7th century. It has remained the same since then without any significant changes. In the regular sacramentary, there are four canons but there are also other canons for special occasions, like Masses for Children, Masses for reconciliation, and two other canons that can be used at any time. The first Canon is the longest and it includes the special *communicantes – In union with the whole Church* and – *Father accepts this offering* ... The second canon is the shortest often used for daily Masses. It is said to be the oldest of the four *Anaphoras* by St. Hippolytus around 215 AD. It has its own preface, but it also adapts and uses other prefaces too. The third Eucharistic prayer is said to be based on the ancient Alexandrian, Byzantine and Maronite *Anaphoras*, rich in sacrificial theology, it focuses on the role of the Holy Spirit and the sacrifice of Christ. It is used mostly for Sunday Masses and some of the Holy days. It accommodates all other appropriate prefaces. The fourth and final canon has its own fixed preface that connects directly to the canon. It speaks powerfully of the history of salvation and of Christ who is at the center of this history.[45] All the canons are purely biblical in theology and in language; they possess a rich overtone of its Latin origins. These words link us to the apostolic Church, the Patristic age, to centuries of Christians who have celebrated this

---

[43] Timothy P. O'Malley. *Bored Again Catholic...* Op.Cit. P. 129
[44] Ibid. P. 130
[45] Charles Belmonte. *Understanding the Mass.* Op.Cit. P. 126

liturgy, offering the same words as commanded by the Lord. These same words, which once were offered only in Latin, are now echoing through the chambers of many peoples and languages to the vaults of heaven. Truly, the Mass and the words of the Eucharistic prayers lift us to heaven and brings heaven down to earth.

In **Pope Francis'** catechesis, he teaches that when the rite of the presentation of the bread and wine have been concluded, the *Eucharistic Prayer* begins, which qualifies the celebration of the Mass and constitutes its central moment, ordered to Holy Communion. It corresponds to what Jesus himself did, at the table with the Apostles at the Last Supper, when "he gave thanks" over the bread and then over the cup of wine (cf. Mt 26:27; Mk 14:23; Lk 22:17, 19; 1 Cor. 11:24): his thanksgiving lives again each time we celebrate the Eucharist, joining us to his sacrifice of salvation.

In the Eucharistic Prayer which is solemn — the Church expresses what she achieves when she celebrates the Eucharist and the reason why it is celebrated; she makes communion with Christ truly present in the consecrated Bread and Wine. After inviting the people to lift up their hearts to the Lord and to give him thanks, the priest pronounces the Prayer aloud, in the name of all those present, addressing the Father through Jesus in the Holy Spirit. "The meaning of the Prayer is that the entire congregation of the faithful should join with Christ in confessing the great deeds of God and in the offering of Sacrifice" (*General Instruction of the Roman Missal*, 78). And in order to join oneself with the praying community, the *ecclesia*, one needs to understand. For this reason, the Church has wished to celebrate Mass in the language that the people understand, so that each one may join himself or herself in this praise and in this great prayer with led by the priest. In truth, "The sacrifice of Christ and the sacrifice of the Eucharist are one single sacrifice." (*Catechism of the Catholic Church*, 1367).

The Greek word **Epiclesis,** which means to call upon, is also known as the invocation. Here the priest requests the Father to send the Holy Spirit upon the gifts of bread and wine placed on the altar so that they may become the body and blood of the Lord. Some writers find a parallel here between the Jews who pleaded with God to send the Messiah. The priest now pleads with the Father that Christ,

He who is Lord, Messiah, priest, and king be made known again, in the Eucharist. In all the canons, the same invocations are made. In canon II, the priest prays; "Make holy, therefore, these gifts, we pray, by sending down your Spirit upon them like the dew fall, so that they may become for us the Body and Blood of our Lord, Jesus Christ." Within the epiclesis, a second prayer is offered calling for our communion as a people with Christ; "Grant that we, who are nourished with the Body and Blood of your Son and filled with His Holy Spirit, may become one body, one Spirit in Christ." The Holy Spirit is the source of Christian unity between the people of God themselves and with God. In the Epiclesis, the invocation makes it clear that it is the work of the Father to sanctify these gifts, the priest symbolically brings his hands together, palms down over the bread and wine.[46] This gesture is repeated at the ordination rite of a priest as the Holy Spirit is called upon the man to be ordained. The actions of the Holy Spirit in salvation history is fundamental to what Catholics believe; by the power of the Holy Spirit, the young virgin conceived at the incarnation thereby becoming *'Theotokos'*. By the same Holy Spirit at Jesus' baptism at the Jordan, the Father shows the world the beloved Son. The same Holy Spirit came upon the apostles at Pentecost as flames of fire, cleansing their tongues to proclaim the good news in different languages. It is the same Holy Spirit who gives life to the mystical body of Christ; the people of God of all races, tribes, and tongues, who by sharing in the Eucharist are truly sisters and brothers of the Lord.

The **Institution narrative** and **words of consecration**.

To understand the words of institution, it always must be put in the context of its Jewish roots of the Passover meal. As it has already been discussed, Jesus took this Jewish feast and gave it a new meaning. Borrowing from the Jewish sacrificial ritual of the *seder* meal and even more foundationally, the establishment of a new covenant. Just as the Passover became a liturgical memorial of God's saving actions of His people from Egypt; Jesus turned the Passover into the Eucharist; a 'new and eternal covenant' that also entails a memorial, an *anamnesis.*

---

[46] This gesture is found also in the Mosaic ritual tradition of atonement. The high priest symbolically places his hands on the head of scapegoat thereby putting on the goat all the sins of the people. Cf. Lev. 16:21)

Take this all of you, and eat of it,
For this is my body,
Which will be given up for you...
Take this, all of you, and drink from it,
For this is the chalice of my blood,
The blood of the new and eternal covenant,
Which will be poured out for you and for many
For the forgiveness of sins.
Do this in memory of me.

All four gospels have a record of the Last Supper, but only Mathew, Mark and Luke have the words of institution. (cf. Mt. 26:26-28; Mk. 14:22-24; Lk. 22:19-20) In the sixth chapter of John's gospel, the entire discourse of Jesus on the bread of life is found. The sacred words of institution bring consecration to live and in turn, we have transubstantiation. Maynard Kolodziej says,

> With the consecration, Christ is sacramentally present upon our altars with his infinite merits, with his dispositions of love and obedience with which he died, so that we may join our dispositions to his, to form the offering of the whole Christ, the mystical Christ, the whole Church, as Christ offers himself with his Church. Thus, as we join ourselves with Him, we have a most powerful means of working out our salvation and of asking help for ourselves and for that of the whole world.[47]

At this point in the liturgy, a substitution takes place because the priest places himself in the place of Christ, as if playing a role. The exception is that he responds in obedience as a weak human to the command, "Do this in memory of me." Von Speyr speaks of this obedience, "if this act were not done in the strictest obedience, it would represent a wholly audacious act of irreverence. Done in obedience, it is an act of supreme reverence... the priest standing in the place of the Son, has himself become nothing more than absolute obedience."[48] These words are so sacred that no priest is at liberty to

---

[47] Maynard Kolodziej, O.F.M. *Understanding the Mass: Revised in Accordance with the New Roma Missal.* (NJ: Catholic Book Publishing Corp., 2011), P. 53
[48] Adrienne Von Speyr. *The Holy Mass.* Op.Cit. Pp. 60-1

improvise or change them in any way. If there were to be changes to the canon of the mass, it can only come from the decastery in the Vatican in charge of the discipline of the sacraments. The "Second Instruction on the Proper Implementation of the Constitution on the Sacred Liturgy" of Vatican II states,

> It seems necessary to take this opportunity of recalling minding the capital principle of ecclesiastical discipline which was solemnly reiterated by constitution on the Sacred Liturgy' "regulation of the Sacred Liturgy depends solely on the authority of the Church… therefore no other person, even if he be a priest, may add, remove or change anything in the liturgy on his own authority. (Art. 22:1, 3)[49]

As it was taught in the seminaries, seminarians are reminded summarily to 'do the red and say the black.' This means, follow the instructions written in red letters in the sacramentary. They give directions for the movement and gestures of the priest at mass; when the priest opens his hands in the orans position, when he extends them over the gift or the people, and when he brings his hands together. The black letters are the words and parts of the mass for the priest to say. In the words of consecration and the words of institution are the words by which the Father's power through the Holy Spirit is invoked, and at the words of institution, through the action of Christ, transubstantiation takes place – bread and wine become flesh and blood of Jesus.

At this sacred moment, the entire Church enters a realm of mystery, filled with the presence of angels and saints. The Church stands in the presence of the Lamb who is the groom of His bride, the Church. At this very point, as the people of God, we are in the presence of the majesty of the eternal Father. Note that at the beginning of the Eucharistic prayers, the priest, addressing and giving thanks to God the Father, speak in the second person plural; we, ours, us. When he approaches the consecration, he speaks in the first-person pronoun; using the words of Jesus personally. Von Speyr, speaking of this moment avers, "At the moment of transubstantiation, everyone

---

[49] Austin Flannery, (Ed.) *Vatican Council II: The Conciliar and Post Conciliar Documents.* (Northport/New York: Costello Publishing Company, 1998), P. 99

linked to the Holy Mass – the whole Church, the entire congregation, the priest, those invoked and those presented to God in a special way – everyone receives his life, conjoined with gifts, in faith and through the Lord. As the host becomes the flesh of the Lord, faith becomes life and the Church becomes a living fellowship in the Lord."[50] It is only one who is ordained that has the power to pronounce the words of consecration as he, the priest, at this very moment, acts *In persona Christi*. Meaning the man priest is in a "sacramental identification with 'the eternal High Priest' who is the author and principal subject of this sacrifice of his, a sacrifice in which, in truth, nobody can take his place."[51] However unworthy as the priest is, Christ consecrates the gifts through his instrumentality, he only lends his voice.

Defined by the Council of Trent, Transubstantiation is taught and understood by Catholics to mean that, under the appearance of bread and wine, Christ Himself, living and glorious, is present in a true, real, and substantial manner, His body and His blood with His soul and divinity. Here is the crux of our faith as Catholics. One believes based on the words of Jesus, the apostolic witness, teachings of the patristics, various recorded and scientifically proven Eucharistic miracles around the world, and most importantly for one's personal salvation. O'Malley speaks of this belief thus,

> At every mass, we are called forth to see Christ present among us in his body and blood. We cannot see it as if we are conducting a scientific experiment. We see with the eyes of faith, with senses formed by adoration of the living God. In the Eucharist, we practice the art of seeing... The practice of seeing with faith is necessary for the entire Christian life... Trained in Eucharistic seeing, to look past what is immediately visible, we were led to adopt. Now, out of what seemed like our death, has come new light. Going to Mass. Practicing this kind of seeing, formed us to look beyond what seemed like pain and to see light shining forth in the darkness.[52]

---

[50] Adrienne Von Speyr. *The Mass.* Op.Cit. P 61
[51] Charles Belmonte. *Understanding The Mass* Op.Cit. P. 139
[52] Timothy O'Malley. *Bored Again Catholic: How the Mass Could Save Your Life.* Op.Cit. Pp. 152-3

There are various voices from the past, men, and women of our faith, who have left us their own testimony as to the efficaciousness of the Eucharist. I find from the fourth century, the words of the great St. Ambrose of Milan (339-397) very powerful, encouraging and strengthening,

> Perhaps you say, the bread, which I brought, is ordinary bread. – Yes, it is ordinary bread before the sacramental words; but as soon as the consecration takes place, that bread becomes Christ's flesh. Let us continue. How can that which is bread be the body of Christ? – By consecration. Of what words is consecration made up, and whose words are they? – Those of the Lord Jesus. For all the rest that has been said previously is said by the priest: the praise of God, prayers for the people, for the rulers, for all others. But as soon as the moment at which the venerable sacrament comes into being is reached, the priest no longer speaks of himself, but uses the words of Christ. It is thus Christ's word, which makes this sacrament. The Lord commanded so heavens were made, the Lord commanded so and earth was made. He commanded so and the seas were made, the Lord commanded so and all creatures came into existence. Behold what power the word of Christ has. And if the word of the Lord Jesus has so much power to create things out of nothing, surely, it must be effective to turn existing things into something else. Therefore, listen, I want you to be absolutely sure of this teaching: It was not the body of Christ before the consecration, but I tell you, after the consecration it is the body of Christ. He said it, and it was made; he commanded so and it was created.[53]

As the priest pronounces the words of consecration over the bread and the chalice, he lifts each up for the veneration of the people. He himself will genuflect reverently. Note that it is proper at this time to look up at the bread lifted up and the Chalice raised up.

[53] St. Ambrose. De Sacramentis, iv, 15 quoted in Charles Belmonte. *Understanding the Mass.* Op. Cit. P.142

There are people who reverently bow their heads or close their eyes. It is more desirable and advised to look up at the sacred host and chalice. When the priest genuflects, you may bow reverently along. Some theologians link this elevation to the saying of Jesus "And just as Moses lifted up the serpent in the desert, so must the son of man be lifted up, so that everyone who believes in him may have eternal life. (Jn. 3:14-15) Also, "And when I am lifted up from the earth, I will draw everyone to myself." (Jn.12:32) It is impossible to miss the connection therefore, between the Eucharist and the cross. In many traditions, at the elevation, a bell is rung to signify the sacredness of the moment. As a young altar boy serving mass with the Irish SMA[54] fathers at our Cathedral Church in Ilorin, Nigeria, I remember people, at the elevations muttering "My Lord and my God!" It is not done everywhere, but it is borrowing the words of the apostle Thomas who, upon seeing the resurrected Jesus, came to believe. This is a practice that I find fulfilling and recommend to everyone. In some other climes, some people use the words of Christ, "I am the bread of life", or "Yes, Lord, I believe that you are the Christ, the Son of God, who has come into this world." These are not necessarily uttered out as the liturgy does not make that provision. It is always good to keep the following three things in mind as the priest elevates the bread and chalice; one, at this moment, the Lord Himself is present on the altar and among His people. Two, it reminds us all to always look up to Jesus (Re: *lift up your heart*). Third, it is an appropriate time to adore and venerate the Eucharistic Lord.

The Holy Father, **Pope Francis** explains this part of Mass; thus, that there is then the invocation of the Spirit, that by his power he consecrates the bread and wine. We invoke the Spirit that he comes, and that Jesus may be in the bread and wine. The action of the Holy Spirit and the efficacy of the very words of Christ uttered by the priest make truly present, under the form of bread and wine, his Body and his Blood, his sacrifice offered on the Cross once and for all (cf. ccc, 1375). Jesus was most clear about this. We have heard how Saint Paul, in the beginning, repeated Jesus' words: "This is my body; this is my blood". Jesus himself said this. We should not have odd thoughts: "But, how come something that..." It is the Body of Jesus; it ends there! Faith. Faith comes to our aid; by an act of faith, we believe that it is the Body and Blood of Jesus. It is the "mystery

[54] Known as Society of the African Missions (SMA)

of faith", as we say after the consecration. The priest says, "Mystery of faith", and we respond with an acclamation. Commemorating the Lord's death and Resurrection, in expectation of his glorious return, the Church offers the Father the sacrifice, which reconciles heaven and earth. She offers the paschal sacrifice of Christ, offering herself with him and asking, by the power of the Holy Spirit, to become "one body, one spirit in Christ" (Eucharistic Prayer III; *Sacrosanctum Concilium*, 48). The Church wishes to be joined to Christ and become one body and one spirit with the Lord. This is the grace and the fruit of sacramental Communion: we are nourished by the Body of Christ to become, we who eat of it, his Body living today in the world.

This is the mystery of communion; the Church is united to Christ's offering and his intercession, and in this light, "in the catacombs the Church is often represented as a woman in prayer, arms outstretched in the praying position. Like Christ who stretched out his arms on the cross, **through him, with him, and in him,** she offers herself and intercedes for all men" (ccc, 1368). The Church, which praises, prays and it is beautiful to think that the Church praises as she prays. There is a passage in the Book of The Acts of the Apostles; when Peter was in prison, it says the Christian community "prayed earnestly for him". The Church that prays, the prayerful Church-and when we go to Mass, it is to do this: to be a prayerful Church.

The Eucharistic Prayer asks God to welcome all his children in the perfection of love, in union with the Pope and the Bishop, mentioned by name, a sign that we celebrate in communion with the universal Church and with the particular Church. The prayer, like the offering, is presented to God for all the members of the Church, living and departed, in expectation of the blessed hope of sharing the eternal inheritance of heaven, with the Virgin Mary (cf. CCC. 1369-1371). No one and nothing is forgotten in the Eucharistic Prayer, but everything is attributed to God, as is recalled by the doxology, which concludes it. No one is forgotten. And if I have someone, relatives, friends, who are in need or have departed from this world to the other, I can name him or her at that time, interiorly and silently, or write the name so it may be said aloud. "Father, how much do I have to pay to have my name said there?" — "Nothing". Is this understood? Nothing! One does not pay for Mass. Mass is Christ's sacrifice, which is freely given. Redemption is freely given. The Holy Father goes on to reiterate, if you want to make an offering, do so, but it is not paid for. It is important to understand this.

This codified formulation of prayer, perhaps we may feel it to be somewhat distant — it is true, it is an ancient formula — but, if we truly understand the significance, then we will certainly participate better. Indeed, it expresses all that we fulfil in the Eucharistic celebration. Moreover, it teaches us to cultivate three attitudes that should never be lacking in Jesus' disciples. The three attitudes: first, learn *"to give thanks, always and everywhere"*, and not only on certain occasions, when all is going well; second, *to make of our life a gift of love*, freely given; third, *to build concrete communion*, in the Church and with everyone. Thus, this central Prayer of the Mass teaches us, little by little, to make of our whole life a "Eucharist", that is, an act of thanksgiving.

The **Mysterium Fidei** follows the elevation; the priest invites the people to proclaim the mystery of faith. There are various short expressions that have come out of various faith traditions. They express mainly the fundamental ideas of the mystery of faith that is provided by the Church from which the people express their believe that Christ is alive, just like Mary Magdalene did on meeting the resurrected Lord:

– *Christ has died, Christ is risen, Christ will come again.*

– *Dying you destroyed our death, rising you restored our life. Lord Jesus, come in glory.*

– *When we eat this bread and drink this cup, we proclaim your death, Lord Jesus, until you come in Glory.*

– *Lord, by your cross and resurrection, you have set us free. You are the savior of the world.*

This acclamation provides a short recollection of Christ's paschal mystery; placing it contextually in its historical form, in its present reality and the future glory it prepares the Church for. Two of the acclamations are based on the text from St. Paul, "For as often as you eat this bread and drink this cup, you proclaim the Lord's death until he comes." (1 Cor. 11:26) Note that until now, all of the Eucharistic prayers said so far, are all addressed directly to God the Father. Now that Jesus is present on the altar, the people acclaim Him by addressing Him personally and directly.

After the acclamation, the Eucharistic prayer continues with the **anamnesis** recalling Christ's sacrifice on the cross. The priest returns to addressing the prayers to God the Father: *"Therefore, as we celebrate the memorial of his death and resurrection..."* (Eucharistic Prayer II) This recalling draws the mind to what the Church celebrates; a sacrifice of eternal redemption. The Eucharistic prayer goes on to the prayer known as the *offering* which consolidates the notion that the Mass is the offering of which Christ offered Himself on Good Friday, an oblation. "We offer you in thanksgiving this holy and living sacrifice..." (Eucharistic Prayer III). The bread and wine, now the body and blood of Christ, unites the entire Church with the sacrifice of three significant offerings of Patriarchs found in the Old Testament, sacrifices which prefigures that of Christ: the sacrifice of Abel, Abraham and Melchizedek. The priest prays "... accept them as once you were pleased to accept the gifts of your servant Abel the just, the sacrifice of Abraham our father in faith, and the offering of your high priest Melchizedek, a holy sacrifice, a spotless victim." (Eucharistic Prayer I) The sacrifice of Abel justified him because he, unlike his brother, Caine, gave the best of his work. Abraham's sacrifice, though redeemed by God, was accepted because in faith Abraham was willing to sacrifice his only son, Isaac. Isaac himself prefigures Christ; he bore the wood of the sacrifice to the top of Mount Moriah. Christ will also bear the wood of the cross to the top of the hill outside of Jerusalem. Melchizedek, the first priest ever mentioned in the scriptures offered a sacrifice of bread and wine, which prefigures Jesus, the eternal high priest's offering of bread and wine.

As the prayer progresses, the priest enters into a part known as the **intercessions.** He prays for all who will be nourished from the altar with the body and blood of Christ that they may all become "one body, one spirit in Christ." (Eucharistic Prayer III) – This prayer reflects on the words of St. Paul, "Because there is one bread, we who are many are one body, for we all partake of the one bread." (1. Cor.10:17). The priest requests of the Father that those who participate in this holy sacrifice may become "an eternal offering" to God (Eucharistic Prayer III) and "a living sacrifice." (Eucharistic Prayer IV). Prayers are then offered for the universal Church, including the Holy Father, the pope, the diocesan bishop is mentioned, the clergy and the people of God both the living and the dead.[55] In the third and fourth Eucharistic prayer, intercessions are made generally for everyone, "and all who seek you with a sincere heart." (Eucharistic Prayer IV), "advance the peace and salvation of all the world." (Eucharistic Prayer III).

The Eucharistic prayer is concluded with the **doxology** – thanksgiving that the people respond to with the great and resounding AMEN! The Amen of the people is significant as it comes to us from the Hebrew word used by the Levites at liturgical services. The priest, while praying the Eucharistic prayer, prays on behalf of the entire church. The people validate this liturgical action by their "yes." According to Belmonte, quoting St. Augustine, this great Amen is the people's signature under the prayer of the priest. This word of validation is found all over the sacred scripture, "Blessed be the Lord, the God of Israel, from everlasting to everlasting, and the people joined in blessing God by exclaiming, "Amen." (1. Chr.16:36). When Ezra read the book of the Lord to the people from morning until night, the people responded, "Amen, Amen." (Neh. 8:6). It is common to find in the epistles of St. Paul, the word amen as a conclusion. (cf. Rom. 1:25; Gal. 1:5; Eph. 3:21; 1 Cor.16:24; 1 Thess. 5:28; 2 Thess. 3:8). In one of John's visions, he sees the angels fall prostrate before God's throne saying, "Amen! Blessing and glory

---

[55] In Ronald Knox's book on the Mass, he almost comically re-states this position in the following way, "So we start, you see, by praying for the whole Catholic Church. And there is only one altar really; that altar behind me is the same thing as the High Altar at Westminster Cathedral, and the nasty little soup box on which, perhaps, some miserable, exiled priest is saying Mass as best as he can, somewhere in Siberia. Only one altar, and the whole Catholic Church is one congregation, worshipping together; all of you as you kneel at Mass here are only specimens, good specimens, let's hope, of the whole Catholic Church, which is kneeling in this chapel, only you can't see it… Mass cuts out time, it cuts out space… In the Missal … the pope's name isn't there, and the bishop's name isn't there; instead of putting in Pius and the Bishop's name the missal says our pope N. and our bishop N. The point of that, of course, is that popes are not immortal, and the bishops are not immortal; they are only spare parts, which can be replaced.

and wisdom and thanksgiving and honor and power and might be to our God forever and ever, Amen." (Rev. 7:12 and Rev. 5:14; 19:4)[56]

At this point, the priest lifts up the consecrated bread and wine, proclaims,

*"**Through Him, with Him and in Him,** O God, almighty Father, in the unity of the Holy Spirit, all glory and honor is yours, forever and ever."*

To which the people again respond in faith by saying Amen!

These words remind us that all that is done and said during Mass *is through Christ, with Christ and in Christ.* St. Paul also teaches this, "For from him and through him and to him are all things. To him be glory forever. Amen. (Rom 11:36)

The people, who were kneeling in adoration, now stand, and the Mass has reached what is known as the **Communion Rite** which consists of the Lord's Prayer, the rite of the sign of Christ's peace, the proclamation of the of the Lamb of God *(Agnus Dei),* the presentation of the Lamb of God and reception of holy communion.

Historically, the Lord's Prayer has been a part of the celebration of the Eucharist from apostolic times. The priest, using the following words, invites the congregation to pray the Lord's Prayer thus, *"At the savior's command and formed by divine teaching, we dare to say…"* From the beginning of the prayer, "Our Father", it establishes our familyhood as the people of God. Calling God 'Father' makes us sisters and brothers of the Lord Himself. This unique prayer, taught to the disciples by Jesus Himself, changed the way in which the disciples within their Jewish worldview perceived Yahweh. Abraham was the father of the Jewish nation and in the view of the Jewish nation; God was too 'almighty' to be seen in such a familiar and family like relationship. (Lk. 11:1-4) In the writings of the great fathers of the Church like Tertullian, Cyprian, Augustine, Aquinas, and many others, they connect the Lord's Prayer with the Mass, and there are suggestions that the petition, "Give us this day, our daily

---

[56] Most of this section depends largely on resources from Edward Sri's work in his book, *A Biblical Walk Through The Mass: Understanding What we Do in the Liturgy.* It has previously been referenced in this work.

bread," is a prayer for the gift of the Eucharist. It is common practice in many places to see people hold their hands extended outwards. It is a gesture of asking humbly from the father of all blessings. As we continue this prayer, we pray with the apostles and the women and men of our Christian history, spanning centuries who also have called God, 'Our Father.'

After the Lord's Prayer, the priest continues alone,

"Deliver us Lord, from every evil, and grant us peace in our day. In your mercy keep us free from sin and protect us from all anxiety as we wait in joyful hope for the coming of our savior, Jesus Christ."

The 'coming of our savior' in the apostolic age could reflect different meanings such as in the second coming or just the presence of the resurrected Lord among the Church. St. Paul uses the same expression in some of his letters, for instance, "…as we await the blessed hope and the coming of our savior, Jesus Christ." (cf. Titus 2:13). Edward Sri opines that the peace spoken of here, *"shalom"* is deeply personal and spiritual. It is not merely an absence of war or violence; rather, it is inner calm, wholeness that comes from faithfulness to God's reciprocal love. "… It is this inner peace that flows into the world through right–ordered, harmonious relationships with others."[57]

The people respond in a doxology of praise to the priest' previous invitation,

"For the Kingdom, the power, and the glory are yours, now and forever." [58]

This response is taken from the heavenly liturgy of the angels in the Book of Revelation as already and previously referenced. Other Christian bodies include it as part of the Lord's Prayer. However, there is no scriptural evidence to support the idea that Christ added

---

[57] Edward Sri. *A Biblical Walk Through the Mass...* Op.Cit. P. 127

[58] This prayer finds a close similarity with the words of King David as he praised God while dying. It is recorded in 1 Chr. 29:10-11; "Blessed art thou, O Lord, the God of Israel our Father, for ever and ever. Thine, O Lord, is the greatness, and the power, and the glory, and the victory, and the majesty; for all that is in the heavens and in the earth is thine; thine is the kingdom, O Lord, and thou art exalted as head above all."

these words to the prayer he taught his apostles. Nevertheless, it is worthy of the Church's acclamation since it connects our praise to that of the angels, and the house of David, the root of Jesus.

We now come to the greeting and exchange of the *sign of peace.* From the Didache, we know this greeting has been part of the gathering of the apostles for the celebration of the Lord's Day. The epistles show that the phrase, "kiss of peace" must have been a common practice from the early Church. Paul says, "Greet each other with a holy kiss." (Rom.16:16). The same expression is found at the end of the letter to the Corinthians and the Thessalonians. In addition, Peter encourages the disciples, "Greet one another with a loving kiss. Peace to all of you who are in Christ." (1 Pt.5:14). The practice is universal in the Roman rite, and it is encouraged to take place exactly where it is now in the liturgy. The sign that expresses the assemblies' solidarity is different from one culture to another. In some places, a handshake suffices. And in some other places, a hug or just a simple bow expresses this exchange of peace. In the work of Aquilina and Wuerl on the Mass, they assert, "The gesture we make –whatever it may be –must be a sign of deeper and more pervasive peace in our lives. We are not just declaring our peace with the person who happens to be in the seat next to us. We make a sign that we are at peace with everyone – even those people whom we may count as rivals, opponents, or adversaries."[59] Both writers conclude that "We place a premium on charity; and with charity comes peace. Jesus made such peace a precondition of a truly Holy Communion. As a follow up to the Lord's Prayer, we cannot fail to see the link when we already prayed, "God forgive our sins as we forgive those who sin against us."[60] Sometimes, we may encounter reticence in others who do not wish to exchange gestures other than wave or nod in your direction. We must realize that there are many health challenges out there. The same person may have a cold or some infection they are trying not to pass on to you. The sign of peace is symbolic of the unity the people will share at the reception of Holy Communion.

---

[59] Donald Wuerl & Mike Aquilina. *The Mass: The Glory, The Mystery, The Tradition.* Op. Cit. P. 185
[60] Ibid.

After exchanging the sign of peace, the priest intones the *Agnus Dei*- the Lamb of God a pre-communion hymn, given in the three times[61] repeated formula.

> *Lamb of God, you take away the sins of the world,*
> *Have mercy on us.*
> *Lamb of God, you take away the sins of the world,*
> *Have mercy on us.*
> *Lamb of God, you take away the sins of the world,*
> *Grant us peace.*[62]

"Agnus Dei, qui tollis peccata mundi: miserere nobis… Agnus dei, qui tollis peccata mundi: dona nobis pacem."

This acclamation goes back to John the Baptist when, at the Jordan, John sees Jesus and points him out: "Behold, the Lamb of God, who takes away the sin of the world! This is he of whom I said, 'After me comes a man who ranks before me, because he was before me.' I myself did not know him, but for this purpose I came baptizing with water, that he might be revealed to Israel." And John bore witness: "I saw the Spirit descend from heaven like a dove, and it remained on him. I myself did not know him, but he who sent me to baptize with water said to me, 'He on whom you see the Spirit descend and remain, this is he who baptizes with the Holy Spirit.' And I have seen and have borne witness that this is the Son of God." (Jn. 1:29-51) We have looked closely at the reference to Jesus as the 'Lamb of God' earlier on. The same sense in which John recognizes the one who will take the burden of the sins of the world on His shoulders is the same sense in which the Church recognizes

---

[61] Edward Sri points out that "This prayer is typically repeated three time: "This echoes other prayers repeated three times in the Mass. In the *Confiteor*… then in the *Kyrie*… the thrice Holy Lord in the *Sanctus*…" *cf.* Edward Sri. *A Biblical Walk Through The Mass: Understanding What we Say and Do in the Liturgy.* Op.Cit. P. 137

[62] Charles Belmonte says of the *Agnus Dei*, "…is a nuptial hymn to celebrate the wedding of the Lamb with his bride, the Church, in peace and unity, as is described in the book of revelation. There, on the altar, the Lamb lie alive, but as if slain. Twenty-four elders are around the Lamb. They are clothed in white robes and crowned with gold. Thousands of angels hymn the sacrifice and triumph of the Lamb. Certainly, each mass is only a prelude and a token of the future adoration of the Lamb in eternity. Cf. Charles Belmont. *Understanding the Mass.* Op. Cit. P. 181

and acclaims the Lamb of the *pasch-passover* of the Eucharist. St. Paul makes this connection in his first letter to the Corinthians by saying, "our paschal Lamb, Christ, has been sacrificed. Therefore, let us celebrate the feast… with the unleavened bread of sincerity and truth." (1 Cor. 5:7-8)

While the Lamb of God is being said, the priest breaks the large host and puts a small piece into the chalice with the precious blood. He says quietly,

"May this comingling of the body and blood of our Lord Jesus Christ bring eternal life to us who receive it."

In preparing himself to receive the Eucharist and aware of his own unworthiness, the priest prays inaudibly,

"Lord Jesus Christ, Son of the living God, by the will of the Father and the work of the Holy Spirit your death brought life to the world. By your holy body and blood, free me from all my sins, and from every evil. Keep me faithful to your teaching, and never let me be parted from you."

Or he can choose to use a second option,

"Lord Jesus Christ, with faith in your mercy and love, I eat your body and drink your blood, let it not bring me condemnation but health of body and mind."

Significantly, in a historical sense, this action goes back to the 'breaking of bread', which traditionally the head of the household broke with his family. The Jews also break bread at the Passover before retelling the story of God's salvific action in redeeming Israel from slavery in Egypt. Following this tradition, Jesus broke bread with his disciples at the last supper, and again at the Emmaus event. The breaking of bread also recalls the body on the cross, by whose death the stranglehold of sin and death was broken. There are various ancient traditions dating back to the seventh century where the bishop, as a sign of communion, broke a piece of the bread and put it in the blood. It is known as *fermentum* while the piece broken is known as the *fractum*. It is then sent to priests in parish as a sign of unity with the bishop and as communion to those gravely ill. It is said that as the yeast binds the dough and makes one whole loaf, so is the Eucharist the bond and sign of unity between the pastor and his flock, and a sign of unity of the hierarchical order of the priesthood. Some others say, "Therefore, the mingling symbolizes the re-union of Christ's body and soul as in his resurrection."[63]

The ecclesia reaches the time of the **reception of Holy Communion**

The priest reverently genuflects, and then rising, he holds the fragments of the broken host together over a paten (or over the chalice) and showing the sacred host to the people, he says,

"This is the Lamb of God who takes away the sins of the world, happy/blessed are those called to His supper."

This again reflects on John the Baptist's recognition of Jesus as the Lamb of God (Jn. 1:29) or the suffering servant of Yahweh found in the prophecy of Isaiah. With the priest, all the faithful at Mass borrow the words of the centurion at Capernaum,

"Lord, I am not worthy to receive you (under my roof), but only say the word and I shall be healed."

The priest self-communicates under both species. And when it is possible, communion can be given under both species to those attending Mass. After the priest(s) receives communion, inaudibly he prays for himself and the people,

"May the receiving of your Body and Blood, Lord Jesus Christ, not bring me to judgment and condemnation, but through your loving mercy be for me protection in mind and body and a healing remedy."

In a situation where there may be **extra-ordinary** ministers of Holy Communion to help in the distribution of the body and the handling of the sacred chalice containing the precious blood; It is important that the men and women commissioned for this sacred role are properly trained, and they are properly disposed to carry out their duties and act in extra-ordinary situations when the ordinary ministers are not available. The priest approach each communicant, lifting the host for the communicant to see, says,

---

[63] Charles Belmonte. *Understanding the Mass*. Op. Cit. P.180

"The body of Christ"

The precious blood in the chalice is presented to the communicant with the words,

"The Blood of Christ"

In both instances, the response is *Amen,* nothing else is to be added. This *Amen* like the previous ones said all through Mass is a universal consent to what Christ presents to the Church. There is no need to thank your priest. It is not his body or blood. Thank him for his priesthood and service to the Church after Mass.

Dr. Hahn eloquently states what the people encounter at the reception of Holy Communion,

> Then we receive Him in Holy Communion. We receive Him whom we praised in the Gloria and proclaimed in the creed! We receive Him, before whom we swore our solemn oath! We receive Him, who is the New Covenant awaited through all human history! When Christ comes at the end of time, He will not have one drop more of glory than He has at this moment, when we consume all of Him! In the Eucharist, we receive what we will be for all eternity, when we are taken up to heaven to join with the heavenly throng in the marriage supper of the Lamb. At Holy Communion, we are already there. This is not a metaphor. This is the cold, calculated, precise metaphysical truth was taught by Jesus Christ.[64]

At the reception of Holy Communion, the communicant can receive either on the palms or on the tongue depending on local practices and the permission granted by the local episcopal conference. Whichever way one receives the body of Christ, care must be taken that no sacrilege is involved. For those especially who receive on the palms, they are to make sure that no particles remain on the palms. No one is allowed to break the host other than the breaking done by the priest at the fractum. The sacred host is to be

---

[64] Scott Hahn. *The Lamb's Supper: The Mass as Heaven on Earth.* Op.Cit. P. Pp. 56-7

received and consumed on the spot. After which the communicant goes back to the pews, and kneeling, (which is recommended), except for physical inability, then enters a communion of prayers of thanksgiving - thanksgiving for the fullness of graces received in the Word, in the Eucharist and the communion we enjoy with the Lord, and the universal Church of both the living and the dead. St. Paul attests to this unity at communion when he wrote, "The cup of blessing that we bless, is it not a participation in the blood of Christ? The bread that we break, is it not a participation in the body of Christ? Because the loaf of bread is one, we, though many are one body, for we all partake of one loaf." (1 Cor. 10:16-17) Priests everywhere should discourage people from leaving Mass either from the altar rails or before the Mass is concluded. They should be reminded that Mass is concluded by the final blessing, with the procession off the altar by the priest and those who have assisted at Mass.

In most places, during communion, a communion hymn is sung. However, there should be some time for silence while the priest returns to the altar after everyone has communicated. Depending on the situation, the priest enters into the ritual cleaning of the sacred vessels. He will put whatever is left of the sacred host in a ciborium and place it back into the tabernacle. He will consume whatever is left of the precious blood. However, if time does not permit, he may reserve the cleansing until after mass. Care must be taken not to forget the cleansing of the vessels by the priest or deacon. This often is followed by another washing in the sacristy at the *sacrarium*- usually looks like a wash hand basin. Because of its usage, the pipes go directly into the ground and not into the general sewage. Meaning that whatever is left in the sacred vessels after the ritual cleansing on the altar is buried in the ground. The priest, if not celebrating from the altar, returns to the presidential seat and invites the people to rise and pray. Always with the same invitation,

The Lord be with you... Let us pray...

The Holy father, **Pope Francis,** in his catechesis continues his teaching on the Holy Mass saying, with this catechesis we conclude the cycle dedicated to the Mass, which is precisely the memorial, but not only as a remembrance, one relives the Passion and Resurrection of Jesus. Last time, we came to Communion and the Prayer after

Communion; after this oration, Mass concludes with the *blessing* imparted by the priest and the *dismissal* of the people (cf. *General Instruction of the Roman Missal*, 90). As it began with the sign of the Cross, in the name of the Father and of the Son and of the Holy Spirit- it is again in the name of the Trinity that the Mass, that is the liturgical action, is sealed.

We are well aware that although the Mass comes to an end, *the task of Christian witness begins*. Christians do not go to Mass to fulfill a weekly duty and then it is forgotten, no. Christians go to Mass in order to participate in the Lord's Passion and Resurrection and then to live more as Christians: the task of Christian witness begins. We leave the Church by "going in peace" to carry God's blessing in our daily activities, in our homes, in our workplaces, among the occupations of the earthly city, "glorifying the Lord with our life". But if we exit the Church gossiping and saying, "look at this one, look at that one...", with 'tongues wagging', the Mass has not entered my heart. Why? Because I am not capable of living the Christian witness. Every time I leave Mass, I must exit better than how I entered, with more life, with more strength, with more willingness to bear Christian witness. Through the Eucharist, the Lord Jesus enters us, into our heart and our flesh, so that we may "hold fast in our lives to the Sacrament we have received in faith" (cf. *Roman Missal*, Collect for Monday in the Octave of Easter").

Therefore, from the celebration of life, aware that the Mass is fulfilled in the concrete choices of those who personally engage in the mysteries of Christ. We must not forget that we celebrate the Eucharist in order to become *Eucharistic men and women*. What does this mean? It means allowing Christ to act within our deeds: that his thoughts may be our thoughts, his feelings our own, his choices our choices too. And this is holiness: doing as Christ did is Christian holiness. Saint Paul expresses it clearly, in speaking of his own assimilation to Jesus, and he says this: "I have been crucified with Christ; it is no longer I who live, but Christ who lives in me; and the life I now live in the flesh I live by faith in the Son of God, who loved me and gave himself for me" (Gal 2:20). This is Christian witness. May Paul's experience illuminate us too: to the measure, in which we quash our selfishness— that is, kill that which is opposed to the Gospel and to Jesus' love — a greater space is created within us for the power of his Spirit. Christians are men and women who, after receiving the Body and Blood of Christ, allow their soul to expand with the power of the Holy Spirit. Allow your souls to expand! Not these souls so narrow and closed, small, selfish, no! Expansive souls, broad souls, with vast horizons... after receiving the Body and Blood of Christ, allow your souls to expand with the power of the Holy Spirit.

Since the real presence of Christ in the consecrated Bread does not end with the Mass (cf. *Catechism of the Catholic Church*, 1374), the Eucharist is *safeguarded in the tabernacle* for Communion to the sick and for silent adoration of the Lord in the Most Holy Sacrament; Eucharistic worship outside of Mass, be it in private or community form, indeed helps us to remain in Christ (cf. *ibid.*, 1378-1380). Therefore, the fruits of the Mass are intended to mature in everyday life. Thus, we can say, stretching the image somewhat: the Mass is like the grain, the grain of wheat, which then grows in ordinary life; it grows and matures in good deeds, in the attitudes that assimilate us to Jesus. The fruits of the Mass, therefore, are intended to mature in everyday life. In truth, *augmenting our union with Christ*, the Eucharist renews the grace that the Spirit gave us in Baptism and in Confirmation, so that our Christian witness may be credible (cf. *ibid.*, 1391-1392).

Yet, by igniting divine charity in our hearts, what does the Eucharist do? *It separates us from sin*: "the more we share the life of Christ and progress in his friendship, the more difficult it is to break away from him by mortal sin" (*ibid.*, 1395). Regularly approaching the Eucharistic Banquet renews, strengthens, and deepens the bond with the Christian community to which we belong, according to the principle that *the Eucharist makes the Church* (cf. *ibid.*, 1396); it unites us all. Lastly, partaking in the Eucharist *commits us to others, especially the poor*, teaching us to pass from the flesh of Christ to the flesh of our brothers and sisters, in whom he waits to be recognized, served, honored, and loved by us (cf. *ibid.*, 1397).

Carrying in earthen vessels the treasure of the union with Christ (cf. 2 Cor 4:7), we constantly need to return to the holy altar, until in heaven; we will fully taste the beatitude of the marriage supper of the Lamb (cf. Rev 19:9). Let us thank the Lord for the journey of rediscovery of the Holy Mass, which he has given to us to carry out together and let us allow ourselves to be drawn with renewed faith to this real encounter with Jesus, our dead and Risen Lord. And may our life always be thus "in bloom", as Easter, with the flowers of hope, faith and good works. May we always find the strength for this in the Eucharist, in union with Jesus.[65]

---

[65] All the excerpts from Pope Francis' catechesis on the Mass in this book are taken from a series of Wednesday Papal catechesis which he gave between January and May 2018. They are available on the Vatican website.

Chapter Four: "Let us go in the Peace of Christ…. Taking the word with us as a light and guide on our path, and the Eucharist as sustenance for our lives' journey."

Jesus said to them, "Very truly I tell you, unless you eat the flesh of the Son of Man and drink his blood, you have no life in you. Whoever eats my flesh and drinks my blood has eternal life, and I will raise them up at the last day. For my flesh is real food and my blood is real drink. Whoever eats my flesh and drinks my blood remains in me, and I in them. Just as the living Father sent me and I live because of the Father, so the one who feeds on me will live because of me. This is the bread that came down from heaven. Your ancestors ate manna and died, but whoever feeds on this bread will live forever. (John 6:53-58)

The concluding prayer, known as post communion prayer or prayer after communion usually reflects on thanksgiving for the feast of the day and generally, in the gifts the Church has received in the Eucharist. If announcements are to be made, it is placed properly after the concluding prayer. The concluding prayer is connected directly with the reception of Holy Communion and should not be broken even when pressed for time. The priest then blesses the people, in the trinitarian formula,

The priest blesses the people making the sign of the cross with his hand and saying,

"May the almighty God bless you, the Father, the Son, and the Holy Spirit."

(On solemnities and holy days of obligation, a longer form of a three-part blessing is provided and may be used as provided in the sacramentary.) The priest now comes to the dismissal signaling the end of the liturgical celebration. Traditionally in the Catholic Church, this is known as the *"Ite Missa est."*

There are various forms of dismissal, but the common ones include,

- *Mass is ended, go in the peace of Christ*

- *Go forth, the Mass is ended.*

- *The Mass is ended, go and proclaim the Gospel with your lives.*

To which the people respond.

- *Thanks be to God.*

When the dismissal has taken place, the congregation respectfully stand and sing joyfully the recessional hymn. This is a time for thanksgiving, for the numerous graces and blessings God had poured on His people through the celebration of Mass. This grace will accompany the people in the coming days. This grace will strengthen the Christian faithful against sin and the power of evil. This is why the Mass is also sometimes referred to as 'food for the journey.' Even though in the dismissal, the priest or deacon will say, "The Mass is ended, go in the peace of Christ", it refers to the liturgical rite of celebration. In a real sense, we are to take the fruits of the mass with us to live fully our Christian calling. Belmonte states in his work that the challenge of the Eucharist lies in the world we will have to engage,

> The real test for our faith and love for the Eucharist comes after the Mass, during the day: in our faithful dedication to our ordinary work, in our generous service to all and each of our brothers, in the delicate fulfilment of our practices of piety... It will speak simply but also most eloquently of our self-surrender, of our sorrow, of our conversion, and of our decision to follow him, when the Lord comes down upon the altar as the priest utters the words of the consecration.[66]

Dr. Scott Hahn lends his voice to the importance of taking the Mass with us in these words,

> After so much that is so heavy duty, the Mass seems to end too abruptly – with a blessing and 'The Mass is ended. Go in peace.' It seem strange that the word 'Mass' should come from these final words: *Ite missa est* (literally, 'Go, it is sent'). But the ancients understood that the Mass was a sending forth. That last

[66] Charles Belmonte. *Understanding the Mass.* Op.Cit. P. 142

line is not so much a dis*missal* as a com*missioning*. We have united ourselves to Christ's sacrifice, we have just celebrated, through the splendor of ordinary life in the home and in the world.[67]

Do not leave early.[68] While there are certainly exceptions to this guideline, most who leave early do not need to and ought not to. We should stay and join in the final hymn until the priest and servers process out of the church. After, still take a minute to recollect what you encountered in this sacred space, place and time. Think of the week ahead and try to figure out many ways and instances by which you can be a light on the world. It is commendable and a thing of beauty, that now renewed by the Eucharist, each person goes to another person and introduces themselves. After all, we refer to ourselves as brothers and sisters. This is another way we can all experience the bonds of our communion with each other and with Christ.

The dismissal is to be understood from the word 'Missa' – dismissal – sending forth. As I have stated previously, the mass is 'Missio' sending forth. The command of Jesus to the apostles before the ascension includes a sending forth, "As the Father has sent me, even so I send you." (Jn. 20:19) Having encountered Jesus in word and sacrament, we have been renewed and reconfigured to Him. The more deeply we unite ourselves with the Eucharistic Lord, the more deeply we are made aware of the commission to "Go and make disciples of all nations." (Mt.28:19) The dismissal is not simply "it is ended" rather it is the beginning of apostolic and evangelizing work. It is a sending forth of a people who will bring the light and goodness of Christ into the world.

Pastoral Suggestions and Guidelines.

Within the Christian world, the question of the real presence of Christ in the Eucharist has been contentious for centuries. There is a huge gap in the traditional belief of Christianity and the Reformation. Martin Luther, himself a priest, did not deny the real presence of

---

[67] Scott Hahn. *The Lamb's Supper: The Mass as Heaven on Earth.* Op.Cit. P. 57

[68] I remember seeing a sign at the public notice board of a Church, which warns about leaving Mass before the final blessing and dismissal. The poster says, "Remember who left early at the first Mass!"

Christ in the Eucharist, and it was not part of his ninety-nine thesis of errors he wanted reforms on in the Church. It is logical to conclude that without the continuity of priestly ordination by the laying on of hands, the gift of valid ordination to the priesthood did not continue in the 'protestant' Churches of the reformation. Therefore, valid celebration of the Mass ceased in the new Christian Churches. The early Christian Churches after the reformation celebrated the liturgy of the Eucharist but did not accept transubstantiation. They celebrated this liturgy as a common meal to call to mind the last supper, without a real presence.

For Catholics, the real presence remains the focal point of the celebration of the Church's liturgy. From the time of Christ and in his teachings, through the apostles' work and the two millennia old tradition of the Catholic Church, the Church believes and teaches in accordance with Christ, that He is truly present, soul, body, and divinity in the sacred species. Scripture attests to Christ's words,

"I am the bread of life. Your fathers ate the manna in the desert, and they are dead... I am the living bread, which has come down from heaven. Anyone who eats this bread will live forever; and the bread that I shall give is my flesh, for the life of the world." (Jn. 6:48ff)

Like some today, the people listening to Jesus were perplexed at His words and did not know what to make of them. Scripture says they were angry and left Him. In our own time, people doubt the real presence, and seek the Lord elsewhere. The real Catholic-Christian must, in faith, acknowledge the limitedness of human understanding and, like the man pleading with Jesus for his daughter's life in the scripture, we, too, must, earnestly plead with the Lord, "Lord I believe; help my unbelief!" (Mk. 9:24) Jesus is very specific and insistent that He is truly present to us in the Eucharist. And when people walked away, He continued His teaching on the real meaning of the bread of life,

"I tell you solemnly, if you do not eat the flesh of the Son of Man and drink His blood, you will not have life in you. Anyone who does eat my flesh and drink my blood has eternal life, and I shall raise

him up on the last day… He who eats my flesh and drinks my blood lives in me and I in him." (Jn. 6:53)

The great founder of the Opus Dei, Jose Maria Escriva de Balaguer, teaching on the real presence says,

> What we cannot do, our Lord is able to do. Jesus Christ, perfect God, and perfect man, leaves us, not a symbol, but reality. He himself stays with us. He will go to the Father, but he will also remain among men. He will leave us not simply a gift that will make us remember him, not an image that becomes blurred with time, like a photograph that soon fades and yellows, and has no meaning except for those who were contemporaries. Under the appearance of bread and wine, he is really present, with his body and blood, with his soul and divinity.[69]

The real presence is not dependent on one's belief or unbelief. It is what it is because the Lord Jesus says it. Nevertheless, to belief, though a supernatural gift, gives room to one choosing to believe. For instance, to choose to believe in God as against atheism is a conscious choice. This choice cannot be explained by pure rationalism because it transcends human reason and exists within the realm of the metaphysical. In a pastoral setting, without faith and belief in the real presence, the practice of the faith is hollow, empty, and graceless.

The Eucharist is a school of learning about the cross of Christ, about submitting to the will of God. Learning that no matter how difficult the will of God may be in one's life; after the agony in the garden, scourging at the pillar, the crowning with thorns, after the crucifixion and death come the glory of the resurrection. Von Speyr expounds on the link between the Eucharist, suffering and glorification,

> The night before he suffered, the Lord was broken as bread. Thus, he gives up his body twice over in a twofold break: in suffering and in bread. The unity

---

[69] J. Escriva de Balaguer. *Christ is Passing By,* # 9 Quoted in Charles Belmonte. *Understanding the Mass.* Op.Cit. P. 167

of the two breakings rests in his willingness to be sacrificed... The unity of his sacrifice is fulfilled, again and again, to such perfection that we are obliged, again and again, to receive in corresponding unity the unity between the sacrifice of the cross and the sacrifice of the bread. [70]

To enter the Eucharist is to enter into the vocation of Jesus that focuses on doing the Father's will. Jesus, the Lord of the Eucharist, beckons on us all, "Come to me all you who weary and are burdened, and I will give you rest. Shoulder my yoke and learn from me, for I am gentle and humble of heart, and you will find rest for your souls." (Mt. 11:28) The same Eucharistic Lord says, "If anyone wants to come after me, let him deny himself, take up his cross and follow me." (Lk. 9:23). To adore the Lord present in the Eucharist is an invitation to discipleship. Such disciples are not fascinated in a cross-less Christianity or one devoid of any suffering. What the Eucharist assures of certainly is, "... I will be with you to the end of the age." (Mt.28:20)

When at Mass, especially at ceremonies involving non-Catholics or non-actively practicing Catholics, the presiding priest should make clear the position of the Church on the real presence of Christ in the Eucharist and who can receive communion. It is a grave matter and desecration if this is not done. While no one can determine what people will do or not do, the priest has a responsibility to clarify the Church's understanding and practices. Whichever way he chooses to make this known, it must be done with caution and utmost respect. In fact, in most places, out of a sense of unity, non-Catholics and non-practicing Catholics are invited to come at communion time for a blessing. They will signify by some gesture, which allows the priest to know they are asking for a blessing and not intending to receive communion. We take heed of the words of St. Paul, "Therefore whoever eats the bread or drinks the cup of the Lord unworthily will have to answer for the body and blood of the Lord." (1 Cor. 11:27) For practicing Catholics, they, on their part, must make every necessary effort to prepare and participate actively at Mass.

---

[70] Adrienne Von Speyr. *The Holy Mass.* Op.Cit. P. 65

Both priests and the people have the responsibility to make the one-hour communion fast, go to confession if necessary, before going to Mass and receiving communion. To this effect, a good examination of conscience is of utmost importance. This tradition is so important in the Church that it is added to the night prayer of the Church and at the beginning of every mass. Unfortunately, this is no longer widely practiced. On the issue of personal examination of conscience, Adrienne Von Speyr says,

> Self-examination is imperative, since it is impossible to proceed from one Holy Mass to the next while taking no account of oneself. Even if one has made a fervent effort to remain and live in the Lord, the need for self-examination does not diminish... A believer may have sinned only in the most minor way, but his forgetfulness, complacency and negligence in self-examination are even more offensive to the Lord... It is not sufficient simply to presume that everything is, by and large, in order and that the Eucharist has a purificatory power over venial sins. What is crucial is that we stay awake and alert in faith.

When we go to Mass, after observing some of the suggestions proffered at the beginning of this work, there is a need for a conscious effort to focus on every aspect of the Mass. Human heart and mind are easily distracted and tend to wander, yet we must learn the discipline of following the Mass at every step to reap the spiritual benefits of the Mass. Pay attention to the readings, and listen to the homily, focus on at least ONE message that speaks to your heart. At the Eucharistic prayer, envision yourself present in the upper room with Jesus; listen to how the Lord offers Himself to you in the Eucharist. After the reception of communion, notwithstanding the thanksgivings and unending announcements and second collections, still keep in mind what great gift you have within you; your mouth is sealed with the precious blood of the Lamb, and you soul is marked by His presence; and be filled with thanksgiving.

Some Basic teachings on the Eucharist from the Magisterium

There are various magisterial teachings, apostolic, patristic, papal and mystic writings on various aspects of the Eucharist. They all are for the continued renewal and growth of God's People in faith and in love for the Eucharist. For instance, from papal writings, three Encyclical Letters stand out: the Encyclical *Mirae Caritatis* of Leo XIII (28 May 1902), the Encyclical *Mediator Dei* of Pius XII (20 November 1947)[6] and the Encyclical *Mysterium Fidei* of Paul VI (3 September 1965).

John Paul II, throughout his pontificate, wrote an annual letter to priests on Holy Thursday. However, on the Holy Thursday of the 25th anniversary of his pontificate, he issued an encyclical instead of his customary letter to priests, addressed to all Catholics: "to the bishops, priests and deacons, men and women in the consecrated life and all the lay faithful". It was the last of his fourteen encyclicals, **Ecclesia de Eucharistia**, published on April 17, 2003. Its title, as it written in the Roman tradition is taken from the opening words of the Latin version of the text, which in the English translation reads as, "The Church draws her life from the Eucharist", with the first words of the Latin translating as "The Church from the Eucharis". John Paul II (from now on JPII) focused this encyclical on the centrality of the Eucharist to the definition of the Church; its mission, and the profound connection between the Eucharist and the priesthood, and the Holy Father's personal experience of the Eucharist. Without belaboring the issue, I choose to abridge this encyclical for our use.

The introduction opens with the words "The Church draws her life from the Eucharist." Since the Eucharist "stands at the center of the Church's life", it is "the most precious possession which the Church can have in her journey through history". The Pontiff regrets that Eucharistic adoration has been almost completely abandoned" and in some places the Eucharist is not always properly honored, sometimes reduced to "simply a fraternal banquet" or "a form of proclamation" or an ecumenical impulse that seeks to express confraternity with non-Catholic Christians which has led to violations of the Church's discipline in celebrating the Eucharist. Therefore, JPII makes known the intention for writing this encyclical; "The Second Vatican Council rightly proclaimed that the Eucharistic sacrifice is 'the source and summit of the Christian life.' For the most holy Eucharist contains the Church's entire spiritual wealth: Christ himself, our Passover and living bread. Through his own flesh, now made living and life-giving by the Holy Spirit, he offers life to men". Consequently, the gaze of the Church is constantly turned to her Lord, present in the Sacrament of the Altar, in which she discovers the full manifestation of his boundless love... It is my hope that the present Encyclical Letter will effectively help to banish the dark clouds of unacceptable doctrine and practice, so that the Eucharist will continue to shine forth in all its radiant mystery."[71]

In six parts, JPII then gives an analysis of the central message of the encyclical *Ecclesial de Eucharist* – a Church born from the heart of the Eucharist.

First, JPII sees the **Eucharist as The Mystery of Faith;** "The Church has received the Eucharist from Christ her Lord not as one gift... among so many others, but as the gift par excellence, for it is the gift of himself, of his person in his sacred humanity, as well as the gift of his saving work. "According to him, when the Church celebrates the Eucharist, the memorial of her Lord's death and resurrection, this central event of salvation becomes really present and "the work of our redemption is carried out." This sacrifice is so decisive for the salvation of the human race that Jesus Christ offered it and returned to the Father only *after he had left us a means of sharing in it* as if we had been present there... In Communion, Christ offers himself as nourishment, which "spurs us on our journey through history and plants a seed of living hope in our daily commitment to the work before us".

Second, JPII teaches that **The Eucharist Builds the Church,** within the liturgical action and outside of it. Therefore, the Church remains in perpetual adoration of the Eucharist even outside of Mass. JPII's argument; The Second Vatican Council teaches that the celebration of the Eucharist is at the center of the process of the Church's growth. After stating, "...the Church, as the Kingdom of Christ already present in mystery, grows visibly in the world through the power of God... The worship of the Eucharist outside of the

---

[71] John Paul II, *Encyclical Ecclesia De Eucharistia*, published on April 17, 2003, accessed through Vatican.va, official website of the Vatican library.

Mass is of inestimable value for the life of the Church. This worship is strictly linked to the celebration of the Eucharistic Sacrifice. The presence of Christ under the sacred species reserved after Mass – a presence that lasts as long as the species of bread and of wine remain - derives from the celebration of the sacrifice and is directed towards communion, both sacramental and spiritual... A Christian community desirous of contemplating the face of Christ in the spirit which I proposed in the Apostolic Letters *Novo Millennio Ineunte* and *Rosarium Virginis Mariae* cannot fail also to develop this aspect of Eucharistic worship, which prolongs and increases the fruits of our communion in the body and blood of the Lord.

Third, JPII sees a connection between the **Apostolicity of the Church and the Eucharist;** The celebration of the Eucharist lies at the heart of the deposit of faith received from the Apostles and must remain unchanged. The role of the validly ordained by a bishop who is part of the apostolic succession is critical to maintaining this unbreakable link. Important distinctions are to be made when considering the communion rites of Protestants, here referred to as "the Ecclesial Communities which arose in the West from the sixteenth century onwards and are separated from the Catholic Church". Catholics must not receive communion in those churches, nor can an ecumenical service substitute for attendance at Mass. JPII unambiguously teaches,

> The Catholic Church's teaching on the relationship between priestly ministry and the Eucharist and her teaching on the Eucharistic Sacrifice have both been the subject in recent decades of a fruitful dialogue *in the area of ecumenism*. We must give thanks to the Blessed Trinity for the significant progress and convergence achieved in this regard, which leads us to hope one day for a full sharing of faith. Nonetheless, the observations of the Council concerning the Ecclesial Communities which arose in the West from the sixteenth century onwards and are separated from the Catholic Church remain fully pertinent: The Ecclesial Communities separated from us lack that fullness of unity with us which should flow from Baptism, and we believe that especially

because of the lack of the sacrament of Orders they have not preserved the genuine and total reality of the Eucharistic mystery. Nevertheless, when they commemorate the Lord's death and resurrection in the Holy Supper, they profess that it signifies life in communion with Christ and they await his coming in glory.

The Catholic faithful, therefore, while respecting the religious convictions of these separated brethren, must refrain from receiving the communion distributed in their celebrations, so as not to condone an ambiguity about the nature of the Eucharist and, consequently, to fail in their duty to bear clear witness to the truth. This would result in slowing the progress being made towards full visible unity. Similarly, it is unthinkable to substitute for Sunday Mass ecumenical celebrations of the word or services of common prayer with Christians from the aforementioned Ecclesial Communities, or even participation in their own liturgical services. Such celebrations and services, however praiseworthy in certain situations, prepare for the goal of full communion, including Eucharistic communion, but they cannot replace it.[72]

Fourth, **The Eucharist is the basis for Ecclesial Communion;** it presupposes a community that it will bring to perfection, a community that requires a life of grace. The sacrament of Penance allows the faithful to prepare themselves for the reception of Holy Communion by unburdening their consciences of sin. Communion must be denied to those who visibly persist in grave sin, and it is only available to the baptized who accept fully the true faith of the Eucharist. A community that celebrates the Eucharist must be in harmony with its bishop and the pope, and Sunday Mass is of fundamental importance to our expression of community. JPII states,

The Eucharist, as the supreme sacramental manifestation of communion in the Church, demands to be celebrated in *a context where the outward bonds*

---

[72] John Paul II. *Ecclesial de Eucharistia.* http://w2.vatican.va/content/john-paul-ii/en/encyclicals/documents/hf_jp-ii_enc_20030417_eccl-de-euch.html, # 30

of communion are also intact. In a special way, since the Eucharist is as it were the summit of the spiritual life and the goal of all the sacraments, it requires that the bonds of communion in the sacraments, particularly in Baptism and in priestly Orders, be real. It is not possible to give communion to a person who is not baptized or to one who rejects the full truth of the faith regarding the Eucharistic mystery. Christ is the truth, and he bears witness to the truth (cf. Jn. 14:6; 18:37); the sacrament of his body and blood does not permit duplicity… While it is never legitimate to concelebrate in the absence of full communion, the same is not true with respect to the administration of the Eucharist under special circumstances, to individual persons belonging to Churches or Ecclesial Communities not in full communion with the Catholic Church. In this case, in fact, the intention is to meet a grave spiritual need for the eternal salvation of an individual believer, not to bring about an *intercommunion* which remains impossible until the visible bonds of ecclesial communion are fully re-established.[73]

Fifth, the Holy Father of blessed memory speaks of **The Dignity of the Eucharistic Celebration;** after expounding on the dignity in the role of the priest, and the communities where Mass is celebrated, and the impact of culture on religion and vice versa, the Pope speaks further, "I consider it my duty, therefore to appeal urgently that the liturgical norms for the celebration of the Eucharist be observed with great fidelity. These norms are a concrete expression of the authentically ecclesial nature of the Eucharist; this is their deepest meaning. Liturgy is never anyone's private property, be it of the celebrant or of the community in which the mysteries are celebrated." He continues, "Our time, too, calls for a renewed awareness and appreciation of liturgical norms as a reflection of, and a witness to, the one universal Church made present in every celebration of the Eucharist. Priests who faithfully celebrate Mass according to the liturgical norms, and communities, which conform to those norms, quietly but eloquently demonstrate their love for the Church… No one is permitted to undervalue the mystery entrusted to

[73] John Paul II. "Ecclesia de Eucharistia," Op.Cit. #38, 40

our hands: it is too great for anyone to feel free to treat it lightly and with disregard for its sacredness and its universality.[74]

Sixth, JPII, known for his devotion to the blessed Mother, and ever the Marian Pope then speaks of **At the School of Mary, "Woman of the Eucharist."** Here he points to the relationship of Mary to the Eucharist and considers her role as a model of Eucharistic faith. He instructs the entire Church,

> If we wish to rediscover in all its richness the profound relationship between the Church and the Eucharist, we cannot neglect Mary, Mother, and the model of the Church. In my Apostolic Letter _Rosarium Virginis Mariae,_ I pointed to the Blessed Virgin Mary as our teacher in contemplating Christ›s face, and among the mysteries of light, I included the institution of the Eucharist. Mary can guide us towards this most holy sacrament because she herself has a profound relationship with it… _Mysterium fidei!_ If the Eucharist is a mystery of faith which so greatly transcends our understanding as to call for sheer abandonment to the word of God, then there can be no one like Mary to act as our support and guide in acquiring this disposition. In repeating what Christ did at the Last Supper in obedience to his command: "Do this in memory of me!", we also accept Mary›s invitation to obey him without hesitation: "Do whatever he tells you" (_Jn_ 2:5). With the same maternal concern, which she showed at the wedding feast of Cana, Mary seems to say to us: "Do not waver; trust in the words of my Son. If he was able to change water into wine, he can also turn bread and wine into his body and blood, and through this mystery bestow on believers the living memorial of his Passover, thus becoming the ‹bread of life'" … In the Eucharist, the Church is completely united to Christ and his sacrifice and makes her own the spirit of Mary. This truth can be understood more deeply by _re-reading the Magnificat_ in a Eucharistic key. The Eucharist, like the Canticle of Mary, is first

---

[74] Ibid. # 52

and foremost praise and thanksgiving. When Mary exclaims: "My soul magnifies the Lord and my spirit rejoices in God my Savior", she already bears Jesus in her womb. She praises God "through" Jesus, but she also praises him "in" Jesus and "with" Jesus. This is itself the true "Eucharistic attitude".[75]

The Holy Father concludes this encyclical with words of encouragement to the entire Church, to place the Eucharist at the heart of the Church's prayer life. Before the traditional sign off by the Pope, JPII eulogizes,

> By giving the Eucharist the prominence, it deserves, and by being careful not to diminish any of its dimensions or demands, we show that we are truly conscious of the greatness of this gift. We are urged to do so by an uninterrupted tradition, which from the first centuries on has found the Christian community ever vigilant in guarding this "treasure". Inspired by love, the Church is anxious to hand on to future generations of Christians, without loss, her faith and teaching regarding the mystery of the Eucharist. There can be no danger of excess in our care for this mystery, for "in this sacrament is recapitulated the whole mystery of our salvation".[76]

From Vatican II, The Constitution on the Sacred Liturgy, rightly emphatically reminds the would be post synodal Church of the ontological and foundational role of the Eucharist in the life of the Church. Some of the following excerpts will elucidate the position of the synodal Fathers,

> To accomplish so great a work Christ is always present in his Church, especially in her liturgical celebrations. He is present in the sacrifice of the Mass, not only in the person of his minister, 'the same now offering, through the ministry of the priests who formerly offered himself on the cross, but especially in the Eucharistic species. By his power, he is present

---

[75] John Paul II. "Ecclesia de Eucharistia," # 53, 54, 58
[76] Ibid. # 61

in the sacraments so that when anybody baptizes it is really Christ himself who baptizes. He is present in his words since it is he himself who speaks when the Holy Scriptures are read in the Church. Lastly, he is present when the Church prays and sings, for he has promised 'Where two or three are gathered together in my name there am I in the midst of them.' (Mt. 18:20) ... The liturgy, then, is rightly seen as an exercise of the priestly office of Jesus Christ. It involves the presentation of man's sanctification under the guise of signs perceptible by the sense and in its accomplishment in ways appropriate to each of these signs. In it, full public worship is performed by the Mystical body of Jesus Christ, that is, by the head and its members.[77]

The Council fathers teaches that Jesus entrusted this great gift to the Church as a perpetuation of the sacrifice of the cross; "a sacrament of love, a sign of unity, a bond of charity, a paschal banquet in which Christ is consumed, the mind is filled with grace, and a pledge of future glory is given to us."[78] Therefore, the faithful, through a good understanding of the prayers and rites, are not spectators or strangers but with devotion enter into the sacred mysteries of the Mass. Full participation at the Mass and a worthy reception of the Eucharist, according to the Council, should influence the lives of the recipients, to such degree that they should live joyfully, be devoted to the Church, seek to serve the filial bond of the communion of the people of God, and enjoy personal growth in piety. The Council fathers also emphasize the eschatological dimensions of the Eucharist, when they averred, "If the Eucharist is the memorial of the Passover of the Lord Jesus, if by our communion at the altar we are filled with 'every heavenly blessing and graces', then the Eucharist is also an anticipation of the heavenly glory."[79]

---

[77] Austin Flannery, (Ed.) *Vatican Council II: The Conciliar and Post Conciliar Documents.* Op.Cit. P. 5
[78] Ibid. #47
[79] The Catechism of the Catholic Church. (Nairobi/Ibadan: Paulines/St. Paul's Publications, 2011), P. 313

CONCLUSION

"Incarnatus est" – he took flesh, and gave that flesh on the cross, and made that flesh food – the mystery of the incarnation sits at the root of the mystery of the Eucharist. Mystery as it is, it is beyond human comprehension. In many ways, mystery is like love, it is felt in the deepest parts of our being; it does not lend itself to comprehensibility by logic or human reason. The Eucharist is what it is because the giver of the gift has told us what it is. It remains what He says it is, whether we believe it or not. The dough of the bread, the grapes of the vine both elemental to consecration yet inextricably links us to the mystery of our being as created beings in God and partakers of the Eucharist. The Eucharist points us to our supernatural destiny – to death. We may learn to die to self on the one level, but then we must learn to be ready for the moment of our natural death to this world. That is the moment we are consecrated for God; we become something different. We become the leaven of Christ, mixed with dough, which rises and becomes the bread of a new covenant. At every Mass, we are lifted up with Christ to God, we hang on the cross with Him, and we are raised to new life with Him for all eternity, all that we are and will be, are made possible by the Father ***through Him, with Him and in Him.***

Epilogue

As it has been stated previously, the Eucharist is at the heart and life of the Catholic Church; 'the fount and summit' of all prayers. In this epilogue, which is added only to this edition, I want to present brief summaries, particularly from the Gospel of John chapter 6 (also known as the bread of life discourse.) In this chapter, we have the words of the Lord verbatim on what the Lord means by "eat my body, drink my blood." Then I will share two very brief Eucharistic teachings from the Patristic age. I will conclude by making a cursory reference to a hundred year timeline of papal teachings on the Eucharist. It is compelling for me to do this, to show the tradition, which the Lord himself handed on to his Apostles, which they witnessed to and handed on through sacred tradition to us today. This consistency is one of the mainstay of Catholic doctrinal tradition, and as we say during the celebration of the sacrament of baptism, "This is the faith of the Church, which we are proud to profess with you in Christ Jesus."

From the Patristic age, here are two of the greatest names of the timer and what they say about the Eucharist;

At a grand table you have sat, now carefully consider what has been put before you, since it is your duty to prepare a similar meal. That table is great where the Lord of the table is himself the meal. No one feeds guest with himself as food, but this is exactly what the Lord Christ does; he himself is the host who invites; he himself is the food and the drink.

St. Augustine, taken from Sermon 129, 1-2

"Pange lingua gloriosi corporis mysterium" attributed to Saint Thomas Aquinas (1225–1274), is a Medieval Latin hymn composed by the angelic doctor for the Feast of Corpus Christi. It is also sung on Maundy Thursday during the procession from the church to the place where the Blessed Sacrament is reposed until Good Friday. The last two stanzas (called, separately, Tantum ergo) are sung at Benediction of the Blessed.

Pange lingua gloriosi
Corporis mysterium,
Sanguinisque pretiosi,
Quem in mundi pretium
Fructus ventris generosi,
Rex effudit gentium.

Nobis datus, nobis natus
Ex intacta Virgine
Et in mundo conversatus,
Sparso verbi semine,
Sui moras incolatus
Miro clausit ordine.

In supremae nocte coenae
Recumbens cum fratribus,
Observata lege plene
Cibis in legalibus,
Cibum turbae duodenae
Se dat suis manibus

Verbum caro, panem verum
Verbo carnem efficit:
Fitque sanguis Christi merum,
Et si sensus deficit,
Ad firmandum cor sincerum
Sola fides sufficit.

Tantum ergo Sacramentum
Veneremur cernui:
Et antiquum documentum
Novo cedat ritui:
Praestet fides supplementum
Sensuum defectui.

Genitori, Genitoque
Laus et iubilatio,
Salus, honor, virtus quoque
Sit et benedictio:
Procedenti ab utroque

Of the glorious Body telling,

O my tongue, its mysteries sing,
And the Blood, all price excelling,
Which the world's eternal King,
In a noble womb once dwelling
Shed for the world's ransoming.

Given for us, descending,
Of a Virgin to proceed,
Man with man in converse
blending,
Scattered he the Gospel seed,
Till his sojourn drew to ending,
Which he closed in wondrous
deed.

At the last great Supper lying
Circled by his brethren's band,
Meekly with the law complying,
First he finished its command
Then, immortal Food supplying,
Gave himself with his own hand.

Word made Flesh, by word he
maketh
Very bread his Flesh to be;
Man in wine Christ's Blood
partaketh:
And if senses fail to see,
Faith alone the true heart waketh
To behold the mystery.

Therefore we, before him
bending,
This great Sacrament revere;
Types and shadows have their
ending,
For the newer rite is here;
Faith, our outward sense
befriending,

Compar sit laudatio.
Amen.

V. Panem de caelo praestitisti eis.
R. Omne delectamentum in se habentem.

Oremus: Deus, qui nobis sub sacramento mirabili, passionis tuae memoriam reliquisti: tribue, quaesumus, ita nos corporis et sanguinis tui sacra mysteria venerari, ut redemptionis tuae fructum in nobis iugiter sentiamus. Qui vivis et regnas in saecula saeculorum.

R. Amen.

Makes the inward vision clear.

Glory let us give, and blessing
To the Father and the Son;
Honour, might, and praise addressing,
While eternal ages run;
Ever too his love confessing,
Who, from both, with both is one.
Amen.

R. Thou hast given them bread from heaven.
V. Having within it all sweetness.

Let us pray: O God, who in this wonderful Sacrament left us a memorial of Thy Passion: grant, we implore Thee, that we may so venerate the sacred mysteries of Thy Body and Blood, as always to be conscious of the fruit of Thy Redemption. Thou who livest and reignest forever and ever.

R. Amen.

The Bread of Life discourse in John Chapter 6

The gospel of John situates Jesus' teaching on the Bread of Life within the context of the multiplication of loaves. It is important to note that even though this miracle is reported in all three of the synoptic gospels, John's account alludes to the Passover leading immediately to its Eucharistic undertone. The reference to Passover meal points to a new exodus of God's people under a new leadership.[80] As the Passover meal and manna in the desert represents God's divine provision on a temporal journey, the bread of life becomes the food that leads to everlasting life. On the bread of life, Jesus teaches;

"Do not work for food that perishes but for food that endures for eternal life, which the Son of Man will give you." Jn. 6: 27

"I am the bread of life; whoever comes to me will never hunger, and whoever believes in me will never thirst." Jn. 6: 35-36

Amen, amen, I say to you, whoever believes has eternal life. I am the bread of life. Your ancestors ate the manna in the desert, but they died; this is the bread that comes down from heaven so that one may eat it and not die. I am the living bread that came down from heaven; whoever eats this bread will live forever; and the bread that I will give is my flesh for the life of the world." Jn. 6: 47-51

And the Jews quarreled among themselves, saying, "How can this man give us his flesh to eat?" Jesus said to them, "Amen, amen, I say to you, unless you eat the flesh of the Son Man and drink his blood, you do not have life within you. Whoever eats my flesh and drinks my blood has eternal life, and I will raise him on the last day. For my flesh is true food, and my blood is true drink. Whoever eats my flesh and drinks my blood remains in me and I in him. Just as the living Father sent me, I have life because of the Father, so also the one who feeds on me will have life because of me. This is the bread that came

---

[80] Jesus is often referred to as the new Moses, as some will say he is Elijah or one of the prophets. However, contrasting how Moses gave the Israelites manna from heaven in the desert, Jesus will have this to say; "Amen, amen, I say to you, it was not Moses who gave the bread from heaven; my Father gives you the true bread from heaven. For the bread of God is that which comes down from heaven and gives life to the world." Cf. Jn. 6: 32-33

down from heaven. Unlike your ancestors who ate and still died, whoever eats this bread will live forever." Jn. 6: 52-58

Then many of his disciples who were listening said "This is a hard saying; who can accept it?" ... As a result of this, many of his disciples returned to their former way of life and no longer accompanied him. Jesus then said to the twelve, "Do you also want to leave?" Simon Peter answered him, "Master, to whom shall we go? You have the words of eternal life. We have come to believe and are convinced that you are the Holy One of God." Jn. 6: 60, 66-69

In the **Catechism of the Catholic Church,**[81] article 3, part two, numbers 1322 to 1332, the following are used verbatim in in the order it is contained in the Catechism;

The holy Eucharist completes Christian initiation. Those who have been raised to the dignity of the royal priesthood by Baptism and configured more deeply to Christ by Confirmation participate with the whole community in the Lord's own sacrifice by means of the Eucharist.

At the Last Supper, on the night he was betrayed, our Savior instituted the Eucharistic sacrifice of his Body and Blood. This he did in order to perpetuate the sacrifice of the cross throughout the ages until he should come again, and so to entrust to his beloved Spouse, the Church, a memorial of his death and resurrection: a sacrament of love, a sign of unity, a bond of charity, a Paschal banquet in which Christ is consumed, the mind is filled with grace, and a pledge of future glory is given to us.

The Eucharist - Source and Summit of Ecclesial Life

The Eucharist is "the source and summit of the Christian life." "The other sacraments, and indeed all ecclesiastical ministries and works of the apostolate, are bound up with the Eucharist and are oriented toward it. For in the blessed Eucharist is contained the whole spiritual good of the Church, namely Christ himself, our Pasch."

---

[81] Catechism of the Catholic Church (2nd Edition) *The Sacrament of the Eucharist,* Libreria Editrice Vaticana, 1994, Pp. 334-6

The Eucharist is the efficacious sign and sublime cause of that communion in the divine life and that unity of the People of God by which the Church is kept in being. It is the culmination both of God's action sanctifying the world in Christ and of the worship men offer to Christ and through him to the Father in the Holy Spirit."

Finally, by the Eucharistic celebration we already unite ourselves with the heavenly liturgy and anticipate eternal life, when God will be all in all.

What is This Sacrament Called?

The inexhaustible richness of this sacrament is expressed in the different names we give it. Each name evokes certain aspects of it. It is called: Eucharist, because it is an action of thanksgiving to God. The Greek words *eucharistein* and *eulogein* recall the Jewish blessings that proclaim - especially during a meal - God's works: creation, redemption, and sanctification.

The Lord's Supper, because of its connection with the supper which the Lord took with his disciples on the eve of his Passion and because it anticipates the wedding feast of the Lamb in the heavenly Jerusalem. The Breaking of Bread, because Jesus used this rite, part of a Jewish meal when as master of the table he blessed and distributed the bread above all at the Last Supper. It is by this action that his disciples will recognize him after his Resurrection, and it is this expression that the first Christians will use to designate their Eucharistic assemblies; by doing so they signified that all who eat the one broken bread, Christ, enter into communion with him and form but one body in him. The Eucharistic assembly is a *synaxis*[82], because the Eucharist is celebrated amid the assembly of the faithful, the visible expression of the Church.

The memorial of the Lord's Passion and Resurrection.

The Holy Sacrifice makes present the one sacrifice of Christ the Savior and includes the Church's offering. The terms holy sacrifice of the Mass, "sacrifice of praise," spiritual sacrifice, pure and holy sacrifice are also used, since it completes and surpasses all the sacrifices of the Old Covenant.

[82] A gathering of the holy ones.

The Holy and Divine Liturgy, because the Church's whole liturgy finds its center and most intense expression in the celebration of this sacrament, in the same sense we also call its celebration the Sacred Mysteries. We speak of the Most Blessed Sacrament because it is the Sacrament of sacraments. The Eucharistic species reserved in the tabernacle are designated by this same name.

Holy Communion, because by this sacrament we unite ourselves to Christ, who makes us sharers in his Body and Blood to form a single body We also call it: the holy things *(ta hagia; sancta)* - the first meaning of the phrase «communion of saints» in the Apostles› Creed - the bread of angels, bread from heaven, medicine of immortality, viaticum....

Holy Mass (Missa), because the liturgy in which the mystery of salvation is accomplished concludes with the sending forth *(missio)* of the faithful, so that they may fulfill God's will in their daily lives.

100-year Timeline of Papal Teachings on the Eucharist

In this section, I have created a hundred years timeline of consistent Papal teaching tradition on the unique position and centrality of the Eucharist in the Catholic faith. These are very concise summaries; otherwise, we would end up with a tome, which no one will read. These section aims to point us in the right direction for your further investigations and readings. Even more importantly, I seek to show that from the command of the Lord to "Take and eat". "Take and drink", *the Catholic Church has remain steadfast in upholding the teaching that the Eucharist is the true body and blood, soul and divinity of the Lord Jesus Christ.* And that anyone who eats of the bread of life will live with Christ for all eternity.

Miserentissimus Redemptor (Most Merciful Redeemer) in the Light of the Eucharist

Miserentissimus Redemptor, an encyclical issued by Pope Pius XI in 1928, focuses on the themes of divine mercy and the role of the Eucharist in the life of the Church and the faithful. The encyclical emphasizes the importance of God's mercy as a central aspect of Christian faith, encouraging believers to embrace this mercy through both personal repentance and communal worship.

Key themes from Miserentissimus Redemptor are the following; Divine Mercy: The encyclical underscores that God's mercy is a fundamental attribute that invites all humanity to seek reconciliation and healing. Pius XI highlights that this mercy is especially accessible in the context of the Eucharist, where believers encounter Christ's sacrificial love. The Eucharist as Source of Grace: The document portrays the Eucharist not merely as a ritual but as a profound source of grace, that nourishes the soul. The faithful are called to participate actively in the Eucharist, recognizing it as a means to receive divine mercy and strength to live virtuous lives. The Eucharist as a source of Repentance and Renewal: Pius XI urges believers to approach the Eucharist with a spirit of repentance, acknowledging their sins and seeking forgiveness. The sacrament serves as a transformative experience, enabling individuals to renew their commitment to God and to embody His mercy in their interactions with others. As a source of Social Justice and Charity: The encyclical connects the Eucharist with the call to social justice. Pius XI emphasizes that experiencing God's mercy in the Eucharist should inspire believers to act justly and compassionately towards others, particularly the marginalized and suffering. The Role of the Church: The Church is portrayed as a vessel of mercy, tasked with administering the sacraments, particularly the Eucharist, to foster a deeper relationship between God and humanity. The Church's mission is to extend God's mercy to all, promoting peace and reconciliation within society.

In summary, Miserentissimus Redemptor presents the Eucharist as a vital expression of God's mercy, inviting believers to engage in a life of repentance, renewal, and active charity. The encyclical reinforces the belief that through participation in the Eucharist, individuals not only receive grace but are also empowered to manifest divine mercy in their lives, fostering a community rooted in love and justice. This profound relationship between the Eucharist and God's mercy remains a cornerstone of Catholic teaching and practice.

Mediator Dei (Mediator between God and Man)

Mediator Dei, an encyclical by Pope Pius XII issued on November 20, 1947, focuses on the role of the liturgy in the life of the Church, emphasizing the Eucharist as the central act of Christian worship.

The document highlights the importance of the Eucharist not only as a sacrament but also as the source and summit of the Christian life.

Key themes include: Liturgy as a Participation in Christ's Work: The encyclical underscores that the liturgy, especially the Mass, is a means through which believers participate in the redemptive work of Christ. The Eucharist's Role in Spiritual Life: It stresses that the Eucharist nourishes the spiritual life of the faithful, fostering unity with God and among the community. Active Participation: Pius XII calls for active and conscious participation of the faithful in the liturgical celebrations, encouraging a deeper engagement with the Eucharist. Sacredness of the Liturgy: The document reaffirms the importance of reverence and proper conduct in the liturgical celebrations, safeguarding the sacred nature of the Eucharist. Ecumenical Dimension: While rooted in Catholic theology, Mediator Dei also touches on the significance of the Eucharist in fostering Christian unity.

In summary, Mediator Dei articulates the Eucharist as essential for spiritual growth, communal identity, and active participation in the Church's liturgical life, reinforcing its vital place in Catholic faith and practice.

The **Second Ecumenical Council of the Vatican**, commonly known as the **Second Vatican Council** or **Vatican II**, was the 21st and most recent ecumenical council of the Catholic Church. The council met in Saint Peters Basilica in Vatican City for four sessions, each lasting between 8 and 12 weeks, in the autumn of 1962 to 1965. It was convened by Pope John XXIII, calling for an "arggionamento" or updating to present the Church's ancient truths to a vastly changing secularized and postmodern world. Therefore, the Council Fathers produced the sixteen magisterial documents, which are significant developments in explaining the doctrines and practices of the Roman Catholic Church. The following are a concise synopsis of the document on the Liturgy with particular reference to the Holy Eucharist.

Sacrosanctum Concilium, the Constitution on the Sacred Liturgy from the Second Vatican Council (1963), emphasizes the centrality of the Eucharist in the life of the Church and its liturgical practices. Here are the key points regarding the Eucharist: The Eucharist is the Source and Summit of Catholic worship and prayer life: The document proclaims the Eucharist as the "source and summit" of Christian life, highlighting its pivotal role in spiritual nourishment and building of community (ecclesial). Active Participation: It calls for the active participation of the faithful in the liturgy, particularly in the celebration of the Eucharist, encouraging engagement and understanding of the mysteries being celebrated. Reform of the Liturgy: Sacrosanctum Concilium advocates for liturgical reform to make the Eucharistic celebration more accessible and meaningful, including the use of vernacular languages. Communal Aspect: The Eucharist is presented as a communal act that fosters unity among believers, reflecting the Church as the Body of Christ. Eucharistic Devotion: The document also encourages devotion to the Eucharist outside of Mass, promoting practices like Benediction and Adoration while emphasizing the importance of the Eucharist in personal and communal prayer.

Essentially, Sacrosanctum Concilium emphasizes the Eucharist's foundational role in the Church, advocating for deeper participation, reform, and a greater appreciation of its significance in the life of the faithful.

Mysterium Fidei (The Mystery of Faith)

Mysterium Fidei, an encyclical by Pope Paul VI issued in 1965, focuses on the mystery of the Eucharist and its significance in the Catholic faith. Here are the key points regarding the Eucharist:

Real Presence: The document affirms the doctrine of transubstantiation, emphasizing that in the Eucharist, the bread and wine truly become the body and blood of Christ, highlighting the profound mystery of this transformation. Sacrificial Nature: Mysterium Fidei underscores the Eucharist as both a meal and a sacrifice, connecting it to Christ's Passion and underscoring its role in the ongoing redemption of humanity. Communion with Christ: It stresses the Eucharist as a means of deep communion with Christ, fostering spiritual growth and unity among believers. Liturgical Celebration: The encyclical calls for reverence and proper celebration of the Eucharist, urging the faithful to recognize its sacredness and significance in their lives. Eucharistic Devotion: Paul VI encourages increased devotion to the Eucharist, including practices like Adoration, to deepen the faithful's relationship with Christ.

In summary, Mysterium Fidei highlights the Eucharist as a profound mystery of faith, emphasizing Christ's real presence, its sacrificial nature, and the call for reverent participation and devotion among the faithful.

Dominicae Cenae, (The Mystery and Worship of the Eucharist), an encyclical issued by Pope John Paul II in 1980, focuses on the Eucharist, particularly emphasizing its theological and pastoral dimensions. Here are the key points regarding the Eucharist - Eucharistic Presence: The document reaffirms the belief in the real presence of Christ in the Eucharist, emphasizing its importance for the life of the Church and the faithful. Communion and Unity: John Paul II stresses the Eucharist as a source of communion with Christ and among believers, highlighting its role in fostering unity within the Church. Sacrificial Aspect: The encyclical underscores the Eucharist as a true sacrifice, connecting it to Christ's sacrifice on the cross, and inviting the faithful to understand its salvific significance. Active Participation: It calls for a deeper understanding and active participation in the liturgical celebration of the Eucharist, encouraging the faithful to engage meaningfully in the Mass. Eucharist and the Christian Life: The document highlights the Eucharist as integral to living out the Christian faith, emphasizing its transformative power in the lives of believers.

In summary, Saint John Paul II in Dominicae Cenae emphasizes the Eucharist's real presence, its sacrificial nature, and its vital role in fostering unity and active participation among the faithful, encouraging a deeper appreciation of this central mystery of faith.

Ecclesia de Eucharistia, (The Church from the Eucharist) an encyclical by Pope Saint John Paul II issued in 2003, emphasizes the centrality of the Eucharist in the life of the Church. Key points include: Source of Life: The Eucharist is presented as the "source and summit" of Christian life, essential for the spiritual nourishment of the faithful and the Church's mission. Real Presence: The encyclical reaffirms the doctrine of transubstantiation, emphasizing Christ's true presence in the Eucharist and the need for deep reverence toward this sacrament. Eucharist and the Church: John Paul II highlights the inseparable relationship between the Eucharist and the Church, stating that the Eucharist builds and sustains the Church as the Body of Christ. Communion and Mission: The document underscores that receiving the Eucharist fosters communion with Christ and strengthens the mission of believers to evangelize and serve others. Call to Adoration: The encyclical encourages devotion to the Eucharist, including Eucharistic adoration, to deepen the faithful's relationship with Christ.

In summary, Ecclesia de Eucharistia emphasizes the Eucharist's fundamental role in the Church's life, reinforcing the beliefs in Christ's real presence, the importance of communion, and the call to active participation and devotion.

Sacramentum Caritatis, an apostolic exhortation by Pope Benedict XVI issued in 2007, focuses on the Eucharist as the (sacrament of charity.) Here are the key points regarding the Eucharist: Eucharist as a Sacrament of Charity: The document emphasizes that the Eucharist is fundamentally about love—God's love for humanity and the call for believers to love one another. Real Presence: Benedict XVI reaffirms the belief in Christ's real presence in the Eucharist, encouraging the faithful to recognize and reverence this profound mystery. Source of Unity: The Eucharist is portrayed as a means of fostering unity among Christians, reinforcing the Church's identity as the Body of Christ. Active Participation: The exhortation encourages active and conscious participation in the liturgy, inviting the faithful to engage deeply in the celebration of the Mass. Eucharist and Mission: Benedict XVI connects the reception of the Eucharist with the mission of the Church, calling believers to live out their faith through service and witness in the world.

In summary, Sacramentum Caritatis highlights the Eucharist as a sacrament of love that fosters unity, invites active participation, and empowers the Church's mission, while reaffirming the real presence of Christ in the sacrament.

Amoris Laetitia, (The Joy of Love) an apostolic exhortation by Pope Francis issued in 2016, addresses love and family life, with important reflections on the Eucharist. Here are the key points regarding the Eucharist in this context: Eucharist as Nourishment: The document emphasizes the Eucharist as a source of spiritual nourishment for families, highlighting its importance in strengthening love and unity within the family. Source of Grace: Pope Francis underscores the Eucharist as a means of receiving God's grace, which is essential for families facing challenges and difficulties in their relationships. Healing and Forgiveness: The exhortation connects the Eucharist with themes of mercy, healing, and forgiveness, inviting families to seek reconciliation and support through the sacrament. Communal Aspect: The Eucharist is shown as a communal celebration that reinforces the bonds of love not only within families but also among the wider Church community. Invitation to Growth: Francis encourages families to grow in their understanding of the Eucharist, seeing it as a call to live out the love of Christ in their daily lives.

In summary, Amoris Laetitia highlights the Eucharist as vital nourishment and grace for families, emphasizing its role in fostering love, unity, healing, and communal bonds within the Church.

These travel through time grounds the foundational elements of the Eucharist from the Lord's time to present day. In the teachings of Francis, Vicar of Christ and head of the universal Church, the Eucharist is the Love of the one who gave Himself on the cross and on the table – as food for the journey and the bread of life. The Eucharistic Christ is the bond of unity among the people of God who form the ecclesial – the body of Christ. The Eucharist keeps the Church in communion with God, our Father, and with each other. The Eucharist binds all to charity, justice, to community and the building of the Kingdom of God among all people.

Oh Sacrament Most Holy, Oh Sacrament Divine; All praise and all Thanksgiving be every Moment Thine.

Essentials of Catholic Doctrine for Quick Referencing

The 7 Sacraments (The Holy Mysteries):

1. To feed the hungry
2. Confirmation (Chrismation)
3. Eucharist
4. Penance(Confession, Reconciliation)
5. Matrimony
6. Holy Orders
7. Extreme Unction (Anointing of the Sick.)

*The 7 Corporal Works of Mercy: *

1. Baptism
2. To give drink to the thirsty
3. To clothe the naked
4. To shelter the homeless
5. To visit the sick
6. To visit the imprisoned
7. To bury the dead

*The 7 Spiritual Works of Mercy: *

1. To counsel the doubtful
2. To instruct the ignorant
3. To admonish the sinner
4. To comfort the sorrowful
5. To forgive all injuries
6. To bear wrongs patiently
7. To pray for the living and the dead

*The 3 Eminent Good Works: *

1. Prayer
2. Fasting
3. Almsgiving

*The 7 Gifts of the Holy Ghost: *

1. Wisdom
2. Understanding
3. Counsel
4. Fortitude
5. Knowledge
6. Piety
7. Fear of the Lord

*Class of Gifts of the Holy Ghost known as Charismata: *

1. Gift of speaking with wisdom
2. Gift of speaking with knowledge Faith
3. Grace of healing
4. Gift of miracles 6. Gift of prophecy
5. Gift of discerning spirits
6. Gift of tongues
7. Gift of interpreting speeches

*The 12 Fruits of the Holy Ghost: *

1. Charity
2. Joy
3. Peace
4. Patience

5. Benignity
6. Goodness
7. Longanimity
8. Mildness
9. Faith
10. Modesty
11. Continency
12. Chastity

*The 3 Theological Virtues: *

1. Faith
2. Hope
3. Charity

*The 4 Cardinal Virtues: *

1. Prudence
2. Justice
3. Fortitude
4. Temperance

The 7 Capital Sins:

1. Pride
2. Greed
3. Lust
4. Anger
5. Gluttony
6. Envy
7. Sloth

*The 6 Sins against the Holy Ghost: *

1. Presumption
2. Despair
3. Resisting the known truth
4. Envy of another's spiritual good
5. Obstinacy in sin

6. Final impenitence

*The 4 Sins that Cry Out to Heaven: *

1. Willful murder
2. The sin of Sodom
3. Oppression of the poor
4. Defrauding laborers of their wages

*Conditions for Mortal Sin: *

1. Grave matter
2. Full knowledge
3. Deliberate consent

*The 9 Ways We Participate in Others' Sins: *

1. By counsel
2. By command
3. By consent
4. By provocation
5. By praise or flattery
6. By concealment
7. By partaking
8. By silence
9. By defense of the ill done

*The 10 Commandments: *

1. Thou shalt not have other gods besides Me
2. Thou shalt not take the Name of the Lord thy God in vain
3. Remember to keep holy the Lord's Day
4. Honor thy father and thy mother
5. Thou shalt not murder

6. Thou shalt not commit adultery
7. Thou shalt not steal
8. Thou shalt not bear false witness against thy neighbor
9. Thou shalt not covet thy neighbor's wife
10. Thou shalt not covet thy neighbor's goods

*The 2 Greatest Commandments: *

1. To love the Lord thy God with all thy heart, soul, mind, and strength.
2. To love thy neighbor as thyself.

*The 3 Evangelical Counsels: *

1. Voluntary poverty
2. Perpetual chastity
3. Entire obedience.

*The 6 Precepts of the Church (The Duties of a Catholic): *

1. To go to Mass and refrain from servile work on Sundays and holy days
2. To go to Confession at least once a year (traditionally done during Lent)
3. To receive the Eucharist at least once a year, during the Easter Season (known as the "Easter duty")
4. To observe the days of fasting and abstinence

5. To help to provide for the needs of the Church according to one's abilities and station in life
6. To obey the marriage laws of the Church

*The 3 Powers of the Soul: *

1. Memory
2. Intellect
3. Will

*The 4 Pillars of the Catholic Faith: *

1. The Apostles Creed
2. The Seven Sacraments
3. The Ten Commandments
4. The Lord's Prayer

*The 3 Pillars of the Church's Authority: *

1. Sacred Scripture
2. Sacred Tradition
3. Living Magisterium

*The 3 Munera (Duties of the Ordained): *

1. Munus docendi (duty to teach, based on Christ's role as Prophet)
2. Munus sanctificandi (duty to sanctify, based on Chris's role as Priest)
3. Munus regendi (duty to shepherd, based on Christ's role as King)

*The 3 Parts of the Church: *

1. The Church Militant
   (Christians on Earth)
2. The Church Suffering
   (Christians in Purgatory)
3. The Church Triumphant
   (Christians in Heaven)

*The 4 Marks of the Church: *

1. Unity
2. Sanctity
3. Catholicity
4. Apostolicity

*The 8 Beatitudes: *

1. Blessed are the poor in spirit: for theirs is the Kingdom of Heaven.
2. Blessed is the meek: for they shall possess the land.
3. Blessed are they who mourn for they shall be comforted
4. Blessed are they that hunger and thirst after justice: for they shall have their fill
5. Blessed is the merciful: for they shall obtain mercy
6. Blessed is the clean of heart: for they shall see God
7. Blessed are the peacemakers: for they shall be called children of God
8. Blessed are they that suffer persecution for justice' sake, for theirs is the Kingdom of Heaven

*The 9 Choirs of Angels In ascending order: *

1. Angels
2. Archangels
3. Principalities
4. Powers
5. Virtues
6. Dominions
7. Thrones
8. Cherubim
9. Seraphim

*The 3 Levels of Reverence: *

1. Dulia: the reverence we give to Saints
2. Hyperdulia: the reverence we give to Mary as the greatest of Saints and Mother of God
3. Latria: the reverence and worship we give to God alone

*The 7 Last Words of Christ: *

1. Father, forgive them, for they know not what they do. (Luke 23:34)
2. Amen I say to thee: This day thou shalt be with me in paradise. (Luke 23:43)
3. Woman, behold thy son. . .. Behold thy mother. (John 19:26-27)
4. Eli, Eli, lamma sabacthani? (My God, My God, why hast Thou forsaken me?) (Matthew 27:46, ref. Psalm 21)

5. I thirst. (John 19:28)
6. It is consummated. (John 19:30)
7. Father, into Thy hands I commend my spirit. (Luke 23:46, ref. Psalm 30:6)

*The 4 Last Things (The Novissima): *

1. Death
2. Judgement
3. Heaven
4. Hell

Bibiliography

Aquilina, Mike. The Mass of the Early Christians. Huntington, Ind: Our Sunday Visitor, 2007 Belmonte, Charles. *Understanding the Mass.* Princeton, NJ: Scepter Publishers, 1989

Catechism of the Catholic Church. 2nd Edition, Libreria Editrice Vaticana, 1994

Flannery, Austin. (Ed.) *Vatican Council II: The Conciliar and Post Conciliar Documents.* Northport/New York: Costello Publishing Company, 1998

Francis, Pope. *Papal Wednesday Catechesis on The Mass,* Jan – May 2018, Editrice Libreria Vaticana

Fisher, Eugene J. (Ed.) *The Jewish Roots of Christian Liturgy.* NY/ Mahwah NJ: Paulist Press, 1990

Hahn, Scott. *The Lamb's Supper: The Mass as Heaven on Earth.* New York: Doubleday Publishing, 1999

Huston, Paula. *One Ordinary Sunday: A Meditation on the Mystery of the Mass.* Notre Dame, Indiana: Ave Maria Press, 2016

Kereszty, Roch A. (ed.) *Rediscovering the Eucharist: Ecumenical Conversations.* NY/Mahwah, NJ: Paulist Press, 2003

Knox, Ronald. *The Mass in Slow Motion.* England: Aeterna Press, 2014

Kolodziej, Maynard, O.F.M. *Understanding the Mass: Revised in Accordance with the New Roma Missal.* NJ: Catholic Book Publishing Corp., 2011

McBride, Alfred. O.Praem. *Celebrating the Mass: A Guide for Understanding and Loving the Mass More Deeply.* Huntington, Indiana: Our Sunday Visitor Publishing Division, 1999

O'Malley, Timothy P. *Bored Again Catholic: How the Mass Could Save Your Life.* Huntington, Indiana: Our Sunday Visitor Publishing Division, 2017

Paul II, Pope John. *Catechism of the Catholic Church.* London: Geoffrey Chapman, 1994.

_____. "Ecclesia de Eucharistia: On the Eucharist in its Relationship to the Church." *Encyclical Letter.* April 17, 2003, Libreria Editrice Vaticana.

Radcliffe, Timothy. *Why Go to Church? The Drama of the Eucharist.* London: Continuum, 2008

Ratzinger, Joseph Cardinal. *God is Near Us: The Eucharist, the Heart of Life.* San Francisco: Ignatius, 2004

Sri, Edward. *A Biblical Walk Through the Mass: Understanding what we say and do in the liturgy.* Westchester, Pennsylvania: Ascension Press, 2011

The Catechism of the Catholic Church. Nairobi/Ibadan: Paulines/St. Paul's Publications, 2011

Von Speyr, Adrienne. *The Holy Mass.* San Francisco: Ignatius Press, 1990

Wuerl, Donald & Aquilina, Mike. *The Mass: Glory, The Mystery, The Tradition.* New York: Image/Crown Publishing Co., 2011